My Nightlife Is 24/7

Turning Tragedy to Triumph

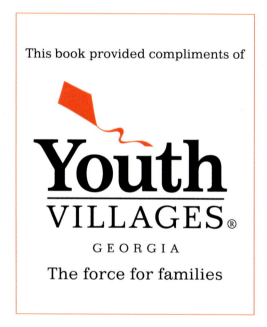
Fiona Page

To Mama and Daddy. I would not be who or what I am today without their love and guidance.

To Christa McAuliffe. Her tragic death and the fellowship in her memory gave innovative teachers an opportunity to inspire youth. This fellowship gave me a reason to live!

To Marguerite and Jack and also to Malcolm P. Dulock, M.D. for believing in me and planting the seed for this book.

Table of Contents

Foreword

I first met Fiona and her mother the summer before I married my wife, Toni. My professional career as a golfer was just about to take off. Her mother, Nana, was an inspiration to all who knew her—including me. Her keen sense of humor made us forget that she could not walk without two prostheses. Seven years later when I heard about Fiona's sudden blindness I knew she must be devastated. Given her mother's example, I had no doubt she would rise above her circumstances.

Having heard about Fiona's success as a speaker and storyteller, we invited her to speak in 1999 at our parent association fund-raising event. Her stories of adversity captivated the audience. Fiona's candor and sense of humor portrayed a woman who was confident and comfortable with her disability.

People often ask the question: How do you find the courage to move forward when your life is shattered by a traumatic event? My answer: Fiona's smile says it all. You don't know the strength God gives you until you have to live it.

This book gives the reader a vision of living in darkness and learning to "see" differently. Her writing gives us a sense of her trials, her triumphs and her vulnerability. Her vivid imagery will evoke compassion from her many readers and audience members where she speaks.

Her story is touching, evocative, and witty. The sparkle of wit Fiona inherited from her mother shines through.

Paul Azinger, PGA professional golfer, sports announcer for ABC network, and author of two books, *Zinger* and *Cracking the Code: The Winning Ryder Cup Strategy.*

Fiona's Notes to the Reader

This book germinated as a result of the many times people have asked me how I lost my sight. What can I say? People are curious. Whether I was speaking to a group of adults or telling stories to children, there was bound to be one person in the crowd bold enough to ask.

The first few years I could not answer them. I was still grieving and much too close to the events to stand on stage before hundreds of people and bare my soul. Time heals. My journey from sighted to blind has taught me many things about embracing change, even when it isn't the change you want.

Helen Keller made the point that the only thing worse than being blind is having sight but no vision. This book is as much about living the blind life as about changing one's perspective. It is about *looking* at what you have and figuring out what you can do with it.

Some people live in denial, which can be comfortable. For many years I lived in denial of my blindness. It worked for me while I silently grieved my loss. Denial had its time and place in my grieving process, but I learned I didn't need to live a life of denial. Thank God.

Standing still in life doesn't work for me. For twenty-four years I've been living with blindness, but I haven't been living in the dark. I have noticed certain changes in my perspective. I began to see people, things, and situations differently, accepting the challenges I faced with new vision . . . a true vision.

My inability to see others' facial expressions and body language really hit me hard. I recall participating in a storytelling class taught by Atlanta's beloved Chuck Larkin. He was a nationally known entertainer who generously mentored other storytellers. Chuck confirmed that two-thirds of communication is body language. The rest is inflection and words. This became one of the truths I told myself to break through the denial to live more fully: *Fiona, you are now communicating with a third of the information you once had as a sighted person.* At first, I was depending solely on *words.* It took a long time before I began to pick up on tone and pitch of voices or refine my other senses.

In the early years of being blind, I felt like I was pedaling hard and fast to stay connected to the world as I tried to interpret the one-third of what I could perceive. But the constant and intense concentration was wearing me out.

Oddly, I can hear much of what my sighted friends can't hear. In contrast, I am limited with what I hear at certain pitches. As I become older, soft voices are almost impossible to interpret. The good news is my ability to separate sounds, like in a noisy restaurant, has improved. Perhaps this illustrates a way my discernment is better.

My sister Sandra laughs at that statement. My family has long debated my need for a hearing aid. "Oh, I don't want to be blind *and* deaf!" That reminds me too much of our Labrador retriever who became blind, deaf, and unable to stand. I don't want to succumb to Trek's fate!

In the summer of 2009, I was helping my sister can pickles and vegetables. We stopped to rest for a while. I was sitting in her oversized lounge chair in front of the TV when Sandra came over and nudged me.

"You want to get back on the okra?" she asked.

"Oprah isn't on until four."

Sandra chuckled. "Yes, Fiona, I think it's time to take up a collection for those hearing aids!"

Can you remember the last time you laughed about a miscommunication? Everyone has a funny story about a time they misheard something or had a communication failure. I've had my fair share. Of course, not all miscommunication is recalled with a chuckle. Sometimes it leads to hurt feelings and resentments. When this happens, we feel disconnected from others and don't understand why.

I have grown spiritually, emotionally, and mentally. You may think this book is about living with blindness. It's more about self-discovery in the face of adversity. Turn the page and you will see these stories will enlighten and entertain you.

My hope, dear reader, is that this book connects with you . . . that it touches you at some deep level, perhaps with a laugh or a tear or even a reflection of yourself.

Fiona Page
Atlanta, Georgia

1

My Nightlife Is 24/7

Have you ever noticed how often you use the words "look" . . . "watch" . . . and "see"? I can't tell you how many times in my presence people have spoken those words, then stopped and apologized because they felt foolish using vision-related terms with me, a blind person.

"Looks like rain, Fiona. Bring your umbrella." Then silence as my friend processes whether her reference to vision offended me.

"Let's watch the news and see what the weatherman says." Then a quick rewording: "I should have said 'Let's turn on the TV and listen to the weatherman.'" I smile and say, "It's okay. I knew what you meant."

"See what I mean?" That's followed by an awkward sputter of words that only makes matters worse: "Oh, Fiona, I wish I'd said 'Do you *understand* what I mean?'" I'm thankful that my friends can usually break into laughter at this point when they realize their attempt to spare me pain just resulted in suggesting I'm a dumb blonde rather than blind.

• • •

Laughter is the best medicine!

At times I've felt awkward trying to put sighted people at ease, but I'm getting used to it. They seem startled when I use those vision words myself. I usually find that the best approach is just to say, "Hey, I look, I watch, I see. I just do those differently."

In fact, if you're a sighted person, I'll let you in on a secret: Because I lost my eyesight when I was in my forties, my speech patterns were already formed using words like "look," "watch," and "see," which is why I find it amusing when someone inadvertently blurts, "Did you see that television show the other night?" or "Watch out for that fire hydrant!" I stifle a chuckle while it dawns on them what they've just said. In fact, I love it when my friends comment, "You look nice today," and I reply, "So do you!" They catch on and laugh. For someone who doesn't know me, that reply might stop them dead in their tracks. I thank God for friends, family members, and others who know me and love me for who I am, including my sometimes wacky sense of humor.

But the fact is this: My nightlife is 24/7.

I am totally blind. What I see in front of my eyes is a blue-gray-black nothingness—an image, if that's what you want to call it, that's not solid or uniform, but more like a piece of cloth that has tiny faded areas. Most of the time the image appears like it contains millions of tiny pinholes. The shading seems to change with my mood. It can be bluish-gray or charcoal, but I don't see shadows or defined objects.

Occasionally I can sense someone walking or making motions in front of me. Some silly person I may have just met might wave wiggly fingers in front of my face and ask: "How many fingers am I holding up?"

"I don't know how many fingers you are waving around."

The darkness is still dark.

Usually I am concentrating so intently on whatever I'm doing or thinking that I don't notice the darkness I live with 24/7. My imagination takes over. This allows me to visualize my life as it is happening, much like watching a movie in my mind.

The blind character played by Al Pacino in *Scent of a Woman* was bold. I am not always bold, although I have been described as such. I would like to be more adventurous like the character Richard Pryor plays in *Hear No Evil, See No Evil.* He was outrageously funny "driving blind." I wish I could be as brave as the character in the movie *Blink.* A blind woman who lives alone is a witness to a murder, and she knows she can identify the murderer even without the benefit of sight, because—like me—her other senses have become more acute. I went to these movies after I became blind, curious how the blind characters coped.

I also heard books on tape. Stuart Woods' terrifying novel, *Dead Eyes,* was particularly revealing. I could relate to what the character was feeling as she tried to become accustomed to her new life without sight. I've been there. She tried to hide her loss as I did at first. Eventually, of course, I made a certain peace with it. At times, such as when I'm enjoying someone's reaction to my complement on her appearance, my blindness is even my friend.

After twenty-three years you would think I'd be skilled at being blind, but the truth is this: In my world of darkness, the learning curve never ends. I can no longer say I'm the new blind kid on the block. I now realize that it doesn't matter if I've been blind four years or forty. My reality is that the unknown is still stressful.

Yes, I have adapted, but in new surroundings I'm still anxious. The truth is that fixing a meal or finding something I have lost still takes longer than for sighted people.

• • •

You may wonder how I cope.

I can't drive so I depend heavily on the man in my life I call Perfect Paul, who keeps me in touch with the world. Like me, Perfect Paul doesn't drive a car, but he does drive *my* world. "He"—a software program for visually impaired people—reads to me in his monotone, computer-generated voice through the screen of my computer. He keeps me connected by reading emails, writing stories, keeping my calendar, whatever I need. He is the only perfect man I know, because he communicates exactly what I request, and he never complains. I still have to press the keys, but I like that contact. And his soothing voice, though generated by technology and not by feelings, keeps me entertained. (I'm also blessed to have help from flesh-and-blood people—including a man who loves me—but more about him later.)

Today I am fortunate to have talking devices that weren't available twenty-five years ago. A scale, a watch, a computer, a meat thermometer, and a thermostat all "tell" me what I need to know.

I don't have devices for marking my clothing or recognizing what's in my refrigerator, but I've designed my own way of identifying colors and packaged foods. For example, I use fabric glue or puff paint from a craft store to create bumps of Braille alphabet to identify the colors of my clothing. If an item such as a blouse features a design rather than a solid color, I attach a tiny safety pin and add my bumps of Braille to identify the dominant color. To identify food packages, I use rubber bands and Braille lettering on plastic attachments which I create myself.

Learning to walk without feeling pitiful challenged me tremendously. I have been so disoriented and awkward that I smacked my shins, bumped into walls, and tripped over furniture. Who knows how often I've cracked my skull or creased my forehead? I have lost count of the number of times I've sliced my eyebrow or put a knot on my head. I know all those injuries sound unbelievable, but they are real. I haven't learned to slow down. My mother used to tell me I had a hard head. Maybe that was a good thing. Just getting out of bed can be risky. Once, I caught my big toe in the top sheet on my bed and fell to the floor. Okay, I know that can happen to a sighted person too, but I couldn't brace myself for the fall.

I have learned to use my knuckles to follow walls, so I don't injure my fingers when I come to a corner. I am trying to slow down and to pay better attention—most of the time. Will I ever *think* before I leap? I want to do things at the same pace as when I was sighted. So many details rattling around in my brain! Concentration is imperative. Focusing for me is a challenge. God did not give me patience for details. That revelation hit me several years into being blind.

My brain still thinks I can see. The most dangerous potential harm for me lies in my body's pre-blindness reflexes. Don't we all automatically bend forward to catch something we've dropped? I have been hurt so many times trying to grab something that slipped through my fingers. Once I got up from a nap and reached over for my earrings, knocking one to the floor. As I tried to catch it, I hit my mouth on the dresser and was sure I'd knocked out my front teeth.

At times my life of blindness has been painful, scary, even dangerous. But it is what it is. I can't dwell on the negative. I am grateful to God for His angels watching over me, and I try my best to stay out of trouble.

When you read what caused me to go blind and its aftermath, you may have a tendency to pity me. Please don't. I am blessed in many ways, despite what I call my 24/7 nightlife. I hope you'll discover that, while I don't have eyesight, I do have vision. I have learned much which I promise to share with you as openly and directly as I can—and in an entertaining way. Trained and educated as a teacher, my profession is storytelling, which I learned and used even before I became blind. When God allowed this journey I never wanted, I began to see how my storytelling could be augmented with books—and my audiences requested them.

So, dear reader, my purpose in writing *My Nightlife Is 24/7* is to share truths I've learned by telling you stories from my past plus stories from those who influenced me most.

My world is quite beautiful. You'll discover why I see it that way.

More glimpses into my new normal . . .

Friends tease me about being overconfident. My friend Shirley asked *me* the date for a party we were attending when she had the invitation right in front of her! I told her in my most confident tone, "It's on Sunday. Gerda's Labor Day parties are always on Sundays."

When we arrived on the wrong day, Shirley exclaimed, "I believed you!"

I retorted with, "You believed the blind one who can't read!"

"But you have an incredible memory!"

"Not all the time, Shirley, and you could *see* the invitation."

How many times have I thought I knew something but had to check myself for accuracy? Like the time Marcia and I were headed out the door for a Toastmaster's meeting.

"Am I wearing my wine-colored shoes?"

"No, they're navy blue."

I bent down to touch my shoes and protested, "No, they're wine!" I was wrong, but so confident I was wearing wine—and not drinking it.

"Fiona, did you forget that I'm the one who can see?" Marcia teased.

I admit it: I am not only impatient, but stubborn and foolhardy, too. Okay, maybe a little overconfident. Thank goodness my friends laugh with me over this.

I look back now and can think of many careless things I have done over the years. Like the time I went outside to remove the deck furniture so my son could build a rail the next day. How foolish of me! He was quite capable of moving that furniture away from his work space. My controlling nature took over. I picked up a lawn chair, thinking I was stepping carefully. I got quite a shock when I stepped into thin air and landed four-and-a-half feet below on the grass.

"At least it was nighttime, and my neighbors didn't see me," I told my son when he arrived the next morning. My guess is he just shook his head.

When my carpet cleaner comes, he reminds me, "Don't try to move any more furniture. Remember the first time I came, and you had already moved the furniture and broken your favorite lamp?"

I was not born blind. I had a normal childhood, raised in South Georgia. I went to college, married, became a mother, and was a successful middle school teacher and professional storyteller. Even before my blindness, life began its upside-down turn.

2
Make It or Break It

When I finished my BS in Education in 1965 I married Bill, my college sweetheart, in my hometown of Blackshear, Georgia and moved that summer to Atlanta to teach third grade. Two years later, Chance (as in "taking a chance") was born.

I was grateful that my child had no birth defects. My mother had been born with two undeveloped legs. She learned to walk on two prostheses without crutches. She was a courageous example to us all, but the fear of it happening again had worried me.

In the spring of 1982, we decided to move to the north side of Atlanta. We found a great lot and put our home in Decatur up for sale. Our house sold quickly. Bill had the appealing idea to spend the summer at Lake Lanier while the new house was being built. Bill was like that—he would put together a plan and expect me to make it happen. Before leaving on a business trip to Sacramento, he gave me a newspaper list of rental houses. I investigated the ones he had circled, and it didn't take long to find the perfect summer home—a brown frame, three-bedroom house with a huge deck overlooking the lake. The private dock for our boat gave me visions of skiing as a family.

The day we moved in, the three of us decided to head down the steep slope to explore the dock below with our eight-year-old yellow Lab, Trek. We were all so excited that we didn't notice Trek had wandered off. By nightfall, we were afraid someone had picked him up. Bill left the next morning for another business trip. Chance and I got in the van and looked all over Browns Bridge Park near our summer lake house and the town of Gainesville. We made flyers and visited the local vet, but no one had seen Trek.

We started the summer hoping our beloved dog would somehow find the way back to his new home. We hit the lake bright and early on Saturday morning. Despite our fears about Trek, those weeks were the best family time we'd spent together in many years. Several of Chance's buddies from his old school visited on weekends. We enjoyed hours of waterskiing and tubing. By his fifteenth birthday in July, Chance was a proficient skier.

Having finished my Master's degree in May, I could relax for the first summer of my adult life. Chance learned to drive the boat. I dabbled in crafts and read. I'd never had so much time for creativity. It was proving to be the best season of the seventeen years Bill and I had been together.

Summer ended, and Chance enrolled in the eleventh grade at Norcross High near our new house. We commuted from the lake until October when it would be finished.

Our last morning in the summer house was heartbreaking. Bill was on a fishing trip. Chance and I just looked at each other that morning. "Mom, what if Trek comes back and we aren't here?"

"I don't know, son." I really didn't know what to say. We discussed the possibility of Trek finding his way back here.

"That would be a miracle."

Strange as this may sound, about noon, the vet in Gainesville called us. Some people who lived twenty-five miles away had brought in what they thought was their lost dog. They wanted him checked out. As soon as the vet looked in his mouth, he knew it was not their dog. He remembered Chance and me from the flyers in July.

"I think we have your Lab," he said as we rushed in. Sure enough, it was Trek! He was barking excitedly and wagging his tail hard. I couldn't believe that, after three months, he had reappeared.

On October 2, we moved into our new home. So much had happened in a year's time. We had moved from Atlanta to Oregon, back again to Atlanta, and then to the lake house. Now one year later we were settling into a beautiful two-story, brown wood and brick house in the sought-after Miller Farms community.

I hoped this move would be our last. We seemed so happy. When we had been there a month, Chance said to me, "Dad is happier than I've ever seen him."

Unfortunately, that happiness was short-lived. Several weeks later, something seemed awry, but I wasn't sure what.

After Thanksgiving I asked my husband what was wrong. "You don't bring out the little boy in me," Bill said. I will never forget those words—what did they mean?

He wanted time off. I asked, "Time off for what?" I didn't get an answer. We argued. We both wanted what we were not getting in the marriage, but we stayed together four more miserable months. He moved out April 1, 1983. People say building a house can make or break a marriage. Ours was already broken before we built the house. I just didn't know it.

I had done all the planning and watched the house being built while Bill traveled across the country for business. I was oblivious to his disinterest. He had always depended on me to handle the home front. I was too wrapped up in the dream home he had offered. Foolishly, I had the floor plans for the house redesigned, giving no thought to resale value. I removed the fourth bedroom from the original plans. We had only one child. What did we need with a fourth bedroom? I had a wall between the living room and den removed without any thought to furniture arrangement. The vaulted ceiling looked great, but I really should not have attempted to turn a traditional house into a contemporary one. I didn't know what I was doing, and Bill didn't care. It was my dream home; it was Bill's "guilt present."

We lived together in that house for six months, then separated, and, eventually, divorced. I find it sad that two people can love each other, but not be at the same place at the same time.

The next two years without Bill in a house I could not afford were lean and lonely. The monthly mortgage was $1,600, and my teaching salary brought home a mere $1,400. Chance found a job and learned to fend for himself. He was very responsible. I credit that to my parents who were wonderful role models. During those two years in the house I floundered, uncertain what the future would hold. I was so lost that I gave little support to my son. Thank goodness my parents were my son's stability—they exemplified determination and a strong work ethic. He spent a lot of time in Blackshear with them.

I was desperate to relieve my house burden. A realtor had shown my house for six months with no luck. I decided to try to sell it on my own. Another six months passed. No takers.

After having the house on the market for nearly a year and with no hope of selling it any time soon, I called my mortgage company and asked if I could make half of the monthly payment until the house sold. The loan officer told me they appreciated my candor. He suggested I write a letter explaining my circumstances and keep them informed each month on the progress of the sale.

"Most people avoid us. When your house sells, we will get our money."

Amazed, I did as they asked. I phoned them every month to keep them informed. The situation was looking bleak. Several months later, a young man called to schedule an appointment to see the house. He said he was single, and it sounded like my house plan was just what he wanted. The more we talked, the more excited I got. I was certain that my basement was crying out for a workshop. This man loved to fix things. *Maybe he'll be the kind of buyer I've been hoping for.*

I rushed upstairs to clean the shower door. When the doorbell rang, I cried out, "Yikes, I'm not finished!"

I pushed the shower door to open it. It was stuck, and I was inside with that doorbell clanging! I jerked it, and the door shattered before my eyes. Why did he have to be early? I picked my way through the chards of glass, thinking that I was running out of money and now I had to buy a new shower door. With tears brimming, I ran downstairs to the door still clad in shorts and barefooted. I stammered as I opened it, "I am so sorry. The shower door just fell. I'll get it fixed." I recovered and flashed him a big smile through the tears, "Let me show you around."

He was kind, understanding, and charmed by the house. He made an offer I couldn't refuse and invited me to dinner the next night. After dinner, we bought the shower door, and he installed it. I know what you are thinking—this is a fairy tale love story, but it isn't. We became good friends. He loved the house, and I felt it was so right for him.

Over the summer I lived with friends while I saved my money. When my house sold, the mortgage company offered me credit for the future purchase of another home. Being a single woman in the '80s meant that qualifying for a new mortgage would not be easy. Yet the mortgage company appreciated my honesty, another lesson in how it pays to be upfront and straightforward. I began looking for a place all my own.

• • •

By fall I'd found a little two-bedroom townhouse. Chance had finished high school and gone to England to spread his wings as a nineteen-year-old. I was on my own. I would prove to myself I could manage my life and provide my own support.

I had been married all my adult life. I was shaky, but I was looking forward to being able to take care of myself. My goal was to start saving money—something my husband and I had never done. I remembered the Human Resources director for Gwinnett County schools telling us that the risk of becoming disabled is much greater than dying before retirement age. I made it my goal to enroll in disability insurance by December. I worked as a hostess at a restaurant, told stories at birthday parties, and taught eighth grade. Things were looking up. I was single, forty-one, and looking!

My small home was exciting to decorate even on my tight budget. Each day after school I couldn't wait to get back on the task of wall-papering or painting. I chose a cool aqua blue for my huge bedroom that overlooked a golf course. I even upholstered my headboard with a mauve and aqua plaid. The walls looked blue in the daytime and green at night. I loved the six-foot sliding windows that stretched most of the way across the back wall of my room. It was so much fun to wake up to that view each morning. I could not imagine that enjoying it would be short-lived.

I met a used car salesman and let him talk me into leasing a car. I did it! I leased that brand new silver-blue Chrysler LeBaron. I was giddy with excitement . . . a new house, new decorating, a new car, and saving money. I was feeling so competent.

There was in fact life after divorce.

3

Love Ain't No Thinkin' Thing

Driving down Peachtree Road on a sultry Sunday evening, August 28, 1985, I chided myself for letting my summer vacation slip by. Was I going to blink and find myself an old woman?

I had been distracted by a summer research job of rewriting the social studies curriculum for my school system. My goal had been to take out disability insurance and pay off debts incurred as a result of my divorce. I felt good that I was learning to be responsible for myself.

My hair was blonde and short. The aqua Capri's and matching top fit just right. The cut-outs on the sleeves had a flirtatious touch. I was dressed in my dancing shoes . . . so primed to meet Mr. Right that I could be plucked like a ripe peach.

Timothy John's was a local bar with a great dance floor—a safe gathering place for middle-aged single women. And it was *the* place to be. I only had tonight to make up for an entire summer. Tomorrow I would be in the classroom with a new set of eighth graders.

In the restroom mirror, I saw a confident forty-two-year-old who was ready to enjoy life. I admired my youthful face, still wrinkle-free. I told myself I needed to take advantage of my good looks. After all, how long could I count on them?

An attractive man caught my eye on the dance floor when his gorgeous blue eyes pierced mine. I felt something unusual. Was this what they called chemistry?

When our eyes locked I recalled the story of my grandmother "making eyes" with the man who was to become my grandfather. They were on a streetcar in Virginia, and she was only seventeen. That was ninety years before my time. In those days it was scandalous to flirt with a perfect stranger, yet I sensed that tonight I felt what she felt—a sense of destiny. Just moments earlier I had boldly mouthed these words across the dance floor: "You're next."

I scooted back to the ladies' room and thought about this as I refreshed my makeup. Was the feisty persona of my grandmother surfacing? I smiled at my reflection and turned to cross the threshold of a new adventure.

I danced back and forth all night with two other guys who were new in town. I completely forgot about my promise to the man I'd made eye contact with earlier. I was just having a good time.

He slipped up behind me, tapped me on the shoulder, and asked, "What about that dance you promised?"

"Ooh!" I smiled, but my feet wouldn't move. Startled, I felt stuck . . . glued to the floor. The momentary spell was broken when he said his name was Jerry.

"This Old Heart of Mine" began playing as he laughed and said, "Well, are we going to dance or not?"

We glided across the floor, and it felt like we'd been dancing together all our lives. We talked as we danced to "Since I Met You, Baby" and "We're Having a Party." When "A Thousand Stars in the

Sky" came over the speakers, he swept me into his arms for a slow one. This was feeling too good.

When the music stopped, I broke the spell by blurting out, "I think I'll go to the restroom."

"Me, too," he said. "I'll walk with you."

We exchanged phone numbers. This was moving fast, but I didn't care. I felt the rush and that was all I was thinking about.

When we reached the door of the ladies' room, he casually mentioned that he had just left home that night; his clothes were in the car.

Red flag! What was he saying? Did he want a place to crash? *Ugh.* I got a quiver in my stomach.

By the time I reached the restroom stall, I'd started second guessing my decision to exchange phone numbers. Sure, he was cute, but I knew I shouldn't get involved with a man who had just separated from his wife that very night. *Fiona, you don't need to get mixed up with one of the walking wounded.* I stared again at my reflection, trying to clear my head.

My words rang true. As I pushed through the crowd, I thought about how I did not need this. Sure, a few hours earlier I'd been telling myself I was ready for Mr. Right. But the truth was I was still recovering from a broken heart. My divorce had been more than a year earlier, but it hit me hard. I had married "in the sight of God" and taken my vows seriously. *Here I am again—same song, different dance partner.* Dancing was fine, but how could I consider dating someone who certainly couldn't be ready for a relationship? He had his clothes in his car, for goodness sake. That comment alone told me he was looking to jump from the frying pan into the fire.

Determined, I walked out to where he was waiting for me, and announced, "You know that phone number I gave you? Please tear it up. I just got over a relationship myself. I don't have any Band-Aids for your heart. Please don't call me."

His mouth dropped open in surprise. He must have been wondering what happened to the woman who was flirting shamelessly a few minutes ago.

I figured he would think about it.

I thought about it, too. I reminded myself that I was clear with him. I didn't need to nurse a man's wounded ego. I knew I was doing the right thing—taking care of Fiona!

Then I started to doubt myself. What had I let slip away? What if he turned out to be the love of my life? These doubts buzzed in my head all week. I couldn't stop thinking about him.

The following week, Labor Day weekend, I called a girlfriend to ask for a ride to Studebaker's, a local '50s hotspot. I didn't want to drive; I wanted to relax with a drink and dance!

The minute I walked in, my eyes locked on Jerry's beautiful blues. He strolled towards me; I was sunk.

"You won't believe this." He was smiling broadly. "I just tried to call you."

Fate clanged loudly. *It's him! It's him!*

We danced the night away and drove to the lake at midnight. It was the most romantic night of my life. The still lake looked like glass beneath the full moon. Everything sparkled . . . it was magical. I threw care to the wind and slipped out of my Capri's, diving off the side of his boat. I had never swum in my underwear or felt so uninhibited.

Dawn was breaking. Jerry started the engine. We sliced through the still waters at breakneck speed. I suddenly thought of my pants. Looking back, I saw them fly out of the boat. We giggled. How could I go home pant-less?

Jerry and I became inseparable, holding each other nightly, playing our favorite songs. We both loved country music and oldies from the '50s, '60s, and '70s. Friday nights would find Jerry and me on the dance floor at Houlihan's. People stood back and watched us dance. In my mind's eye, I can still see us dancing to "The Lion Sleeps Tonight."

By Christmas the relationship was solid. Beginnings are beautiful, aren't they? The trust I felt was what impressed me the most. I was liked and loved for who I was. This was a first!

We both had obligations to go home and visit our parents for the holidays, and we had mixed feelings. We really wanted to be together. Holidays are hard on people who are newly divorced.

The night before Christmas we sat on the floor, dreading the moment we would go our separate ways. Jerry said, "Go ahead and open your gift."

I opened it, revealing his excellent taste. The earrings were triple gold wires for my pierced ears. I loved them.

He had a card for me, and I had one for him. I tore mine open, and gasped, "Open yours!"

We had given each other the very same card and written on it, "I love you."

Our destiny was sealed.

"Love Ain't No Thinkin' Thing" is the title of a song written by a friend of mine. Looking back with more maturity as I write today, I realize that love *should* be a thinking thing. Too often we operate from our feelings, which by definition are fleeting and don't form a solid foundation for the commitment of marriage.

I met Jerry at a time when I was still reeling from the pain of my first marriage, and—truth be told—I had a lot of growing up to do. As I would learn, Jerry loves to serve, to help, and to care for me. Little did we know how important those qualities would become. He is cautious, methodical, and sometimes thinks too much inside the box for my personality, although I admit he has done a lot of mellowing in the twenty-six years I have known him. He and I are both headstrong first-borns.

Our relationship has taken a lot of turns over the years, including one I guarantee you will not see coming.

4

Wildcat Talespinners

Let's backtrack a bit. If you've heard me speak or visited my website, you know I'm a storyteller. By that I don't just mean I love to tell stories—although that's true too. I mean I am a professional storyteller. In fact, my first book is a children's tale, *Bettina the Bold*. It's about a blind butterfly who discovers how to make friends.

Yes, it's a book for children. However, I happen to agree with the late, brilliant author, C.S. Lewis, who penned *The Chronicles of Narnia*, among many other books. He believed that "a book worth reading only in childhood is not worth reading even then." So I'm pleased to say that *Bettina the Bold* has a strong enough storyline and characters with sufficient color and depth to hold the attention of adult readers too. Besides being fun, it teaches values. It took me a while to learn and develop the storytelling techniques which make *Bettina* effective for all ages.

• • •

My professional interest in storytelling as a communication medium dates back to the end of my marriage to Bill. I took a course in storytelling and realized how the techniques I learned would compliment my career as a teacher. It also gave me a diversion while my heart was healing from the devastation of a broken marriage.

When the course ended, I began volunteering as a storyteller to practice my craft at the local library. The story time was so popular that the *Gwinnett County News* did a front page article about it. After it ran, my principal called me into his office. I half expected him to tell me I was in trouble for moonlighting. Instead, he suggested I create a storytelling course for eighth graders. I liked the idea. I had read about Robert Rubenstein, a middle school teacher from California who developed a similar course. I contacted him, got some ideas, became inspired, and designed my own course.

I taught storytelling as an elective while teaching American History to eighth graders at a school whose mascot was the Wildcat. We formed a troupe and called them the Wildcat Talespinners. These students learned how to be better listeners, how to relate to each other, and how to think and speak on their feet.

Now I'll let you in on a secret: My dedication to storytelling is why I chose to write this book as a series of personal anecdotes. I hope you can learn from someone who has found vision, although blind, and who has found the Source of strength, although physically disabled. I've figured out that I'm not meant to be a lecturer or a preacher, although at times I have been considered an "authoritarian" teacher. Even before I developed skills as a professional storyteller, I was using story to teach. After years of being asked to supplement my public appearances with a book, I finally took the hint and wrote one. You're holding it now. So enjoy these lessons from slices of my life.

As I look back on those days as a middle-school teacher, I marvel at how non-readers, bullies, and shy kids caught the joy of hearing and telling stories. Wildcat Talespinners was truly a positive experience.

My classroom became a place where everyone could feel a sense of belonging and let their true selves shine.

In the fall of 1987, I was given a new position—storytelling teacher for the entire middle school. I designed classes on technique, Story Theater, and advanced performance skills. This was a unique idea for Georgia schools. In fact, I was one of only two full-time storytelling teachers in the nation.

Early that summer my principal was transferred to another school. When I heard about this, I thought I needed to pay a visit to the school to meet the new principal, fearing that this administrator might not see the value of storytelling. I dropped by to meet him on my way to the Children's Literature Conference at the University of Georgia. My goal was to impress him enough to secure my job. When I told him about what I taught and how I had assisted in writing the county drama curriculum that summer, he appeared interested—so interested that he handed me an application for the prestigious Christa McAuliffe Fellowship. He suggested I apply for this national grant. The application had come in after the teachers had gone home for the summer. The deadline for entry was July 30—only one week after this impromptu meeting.

Talk about being in the right place at the right time! This was the first year that Congress had set aside $2.8 million to honor Christa McAuliffe. She was the first teacher, as well as the first civilian, to be selected for space travel. I remembered that fateful day when Christa McAuliffe and her colleagues died on the Space Shuttle *Challenger* mission in 1986. Winning this award seemed like an unrealistic expectation, but I didn't want to disappoint my new boss by not even trying.

I trudged over to the school library and used a computer for the very first time. It was the last week in July. The school was empty. The computer was a foreign object to me. I had to call the media specialist to find out how to turn it on. A computer had been in my classroom for two years, but I had refused to touch it. One genius kid pestered me all the time to use that computer. I never thought to ask him to teach me how.

I watched this Apple computer with its funny apple-like mouth edit my ideas. I learned how to make the apple eat the words and that was it. I didn't even know the word "mouse." And I certainly didn't know how to use a tool called "spell check."

I hand-delivered the application to the Georgia State Capitol Friday, July 30. I barely got it in before the deadline and didn't think I had the slightest chance of winning the grant award. That evening I went home to my little deck and reflected on the day after the *Challenger* tragedy. I remembered riding around in my car listening to the radio. Schools were closed because of the space shuttle disaster. I remembered it well. The entire United States was in shock. It was the kind of day when everyone remembers where they were when they heard the tragic news. We teachers felt we had lost one of our own. It was a solemn day.

As I sat there dreaming "what if . . ." I thought about how I could travel the state sharing my passion. I could show educators the value of storytelling in the classroom. It could also be an excellent way to help kids become more comfortable with making a presentation. I could share how storytelling skills can build anyone's confidence—students *and* teachers.

I allowed my mind to dream and plan. What kind of stories would I use if I were a math teacher? A PE teacher? What would I do in an Art class? Think how much more interesting social studies and health classes could be if we shared stories of famous people or even not-so-famous people, and how they dealt with their life challenges. Everybody loves a good story. Students don't get enough opportunities to speak on their feet, to shine, to share. I had eighth graders in my class who were chronically truant until the semester they had storytelling. It was a chance for the one who acted out in class to show off appropriately. I believed every teacher needed to be skilled in telling stories because the current generation was constantly being entertained by television. My job was to convince other educators. Is it not true we best remember a point when told through a story?

I was so enthusiastic. Now my application was more than something I did to please my new boss. If I could win that fellowship, it might open up possibilities for a new career. I could see more clearly what my future might hold. My disappointment of losing the distinction of Teacher of the Year for my school to a popular and dear colleague had stung. However, I had won the DAR American History award for Teacher of the Year.

Who knows? I thought. I could even become a nationally-known professional storyteller. I could travel the world telling stories and teaching others the art. If I continued to be debt-free, then the next summer I could travel the thirteen original colonies which I had told stories about or go to the Grand Canyon and collect new stories to tell. It had been my secret desire to be brave enough to travel the country alone. This was an opportunity for recreating my life.

Little did I know the journey I was about to take.

5

Got the World by the Tale

The phone was ringing when I opened the door to my townhouse. I ran upstairs to my little office on the second floor landing and grabbed the phone. The voice at the other end said, "This is the State Office of Educational Standards. Are you Fiona Page?"

"Yes," I replied, not knowing what this was about.

"We are pleased to notify you that you are Georgia's first recipient of the Christa McAuliffe Fellowship. You will receive a grant of $25,000 to complete your innovative project on storytelling." It sounded like a Publisher's Clearing House call to me. I could not believe my ears.

I dropped to my seat, dumbstruck.

"What did you say?"

The woman repeated the words, adding that there were two recipients per state—one to receive $25,000 and the second for $10,000. I had just turned in the application three days earlier, barely making the deadline and only briefly considering the possibility of winning. After all, Christa McAuliffe was a science teacher, and I taught history.

I shook myself back to the reality of the phone call.

Unsure if I heard correctly, I asked, "Did you say I won the $10,000 grant?"

"No, ma'am, you are the first place winner of $25,000. Your design was selected, because it was such a unique concept for a middle school."

Twenty-five thousand dollars? How could I spend that much money on storytelling? But I dared not say that.

The next few months would be preparation for a tour of schools throughout Georgia to train teachers in using the art of storytelling as a teaching tool. My tour was to begin in January, which meant I would remain in the classroom for the next semester.

A month later, wanting nothing to interfere with my travel, I decided to find the cause of a nagging intermittent pain in my groin. I was fatigued though my family physician had treated me for pernicious anemia earlier that summer. Now I wondered if the fatigue and the ongoing pain were related. When I was nineteen, I worked as a nurse's aide and a still vivid memory was a cancer patient's grim death. Years later, my imagination was running wild. Could the pooch in my thirty-five-year-old appendectomy scar be a hernia or even the start of something worse? My family doc had not expressed concern. I'd finished my B12 shots yet the pain persisted.

Earlier that summer, Jerry and I had become acquainted with a surgical nurse we met at Timothy John's. I'll call her Diane. She was an attractive brunette who was maybe an inch shorter than me. It was so easy to talk to her. She shared a lot about working and being friends with her doctor colleagues. I picked her brain about my symptoms.

Diane told me about a surgeon she worked with in the operating room who had performed a hysterectomy and a tummy tuck on *her*—both procedures for the price of one. I thought that sounded unusual, yet the fact that she not only worked with him but also had been a patient of his boosted my confidence in what she was saying.

"Wow! Maybe I should get his opinion." Since my teen years, I had despised my round belly, like some women hate their flat chests or big breasts. My cousin had a tummy tuck without any complications. Meeting Diane gave me an excuse for a second opinion.

I wasn't seeking a tummy tuck, but I felt privileged to be learning the inside scoop from Diane, as if knowledge of doctors on a personal level puts you in some kind of special sorority. Diane told me her surgeon might suggest liposuction, a new cosmetic procedure. It sounded safe and noninvasive—just a syringe under the skin to suck out all that fat, she explained.

A week or so later I remarked to Jerry, "Isn't it great I met Diane . . . a surgical nurse who can give me expert advice about what doctor to choose?"

Jerry was skeptical. "What's wrong with accepting your family doctor's opinion that there's no hernia?"

"Then how do you explain the pain in my abdomen?"

Jerry had no response.

"Just think, maybe he could do something about the appendectomy scars on my belly—and make my tummy flatter—while taking care of the hernia. I would look better."

"If you want to look better, exercise!"

All that talk from Jerry went in one ear and out the other. I made an appointment with the surgeon. I was in a trance and moving on a track that I could not—or did not—stop.

While sitting in the new doctor's waiting room, I noticed that his business card read: "Plastic Surgeon." It also had DO (Doctor of Osteopathy) after his name, a title I knew to be different from MD (Medical Doctor). I suppressed my doubts.

The first thing I noticed when the doctor strode into the examining room was the cut of his suit and the softness of his loafers. *Odd.* I thought Armani suits and fancy Gucci loafers were for cocktail parties, not what a surgeon would wear on the job. His demeanor was unusual, too. It seemed like he was primed for a sales presentation.

He poked and prodded. He didn't ask me about the B12 shots I had been taking all summer. I didn't think to point that out either . . . I had written about my pernicious anemia in the medical history.

Deciding that I probably did have a hernia, he scheduled me for hernia repair. Just like Diane predicted, he brought up liposuction. "Why don't we do some liposuction while we're in there? We could take off a little here and a little there," he said, pointing to my abdomen and the cellulite on my hips. "Suck a little above the pubic bone, a little on the hips. Very simple and it won't cost you any more. Your insurance will cover everything."

Since it was exactly what Diane told me he would say, I was primed to agree. I heard myself murmur, "Yes," never letting my doubts surface.

That evening I told Jerry about the visit with the doctor and the plan for liposuction.

"No," he said emphatically. "What you need is exercise!"

I dug in my heels, deciding Jerry was being insensitive. "I have never had a flat tummy. I would look better!" I said no more, determined to do what I wanted.

The next day when I went in to have my blood work done the medical assistant shoved some blank medical forms in front of me. "Why am I signing blank forms? What are these for?"

She explained they were standard procedural forms for surgery and that the doctor hadn't come by yet. "This gives the doctor permission to do what he deems necessary once he sees the situation inside. He will stop by the office later."

"Okay," I said, thinking that sounded reasonable. A doctor is under Hippocratic Oath to keep his patient from harm at all cost—the physician's solemn vow to do the right thing. I signed the blank forms.

The next morning, with Jerry by my side, I was admitted to the hospital as an outpatient. The plastic surgeon strolled into my room with his magic marker and demonstrated the locations for the liposuction.

Jerry walked out.

When he returned, he said, "I thought you weren't going to do that."

I snapped back with: "It's my decision."

Jerry just looked at me for a second and turned quickly—walking away without another word.

Several hours later I awoke in the recovery room to the face of another physician, who said, "I am the bearer of bad news."

"What do you mean? Where's my doctor?"

"Oh, he's out of town."

That was quick, I thought.

The doctor continued, "Well, the good news is we did not find a hernia. The bad news is that you've had a major laparotomy. You'll be out of work for six weeks instead of ten days."

"Why?"

"He was searching for the pain you described."

I've had my stomach cut open for nothing! A cut like a Caesarean!

"Oh, no, not six weeks! I told my boss I'd be out for only ten days." No qualified substitute was available to teach my class on storytelling techniques. Would other teachers have to pick up the overload? If not, I wondered what my kids were going to do. Stare at the walls?

I was sent home from the hospital with a prescription for pain and some written instructions prepared by the surgeon. In his haste to leave town, he had failed to write complete discharge instructions. He did not warn me about the increased risks for blood clots following surgery. Later I would learn that, without a prescription for surgical stockings and strict instructions to remain active, I was in danger of developing a deadly blood clot. I also would discover that my doctor never picked up the pre-op lab report, which indicated I was anemic. Performing unnecessary surgery on an anemic person should have been out of the question.

Although I did not know these medical details when I left the hospital, I was still so distressed about the outcome of the surgery that I slept most of the next three days. When I got up on Tuesday my thigh was painfully swollen, so I went back to bed feeling even more depressed.

In the early morning hours, I woke with a sharp pain on the inside of my left thigh. The pain was so intense I thought it was a "Charley horse." By mid-morning it was burning hot. By the end of the next day, I could see that my leg was twice the size of the other leg so I called the doctor's office. The receptionist told me she would get back with me. I heard from her about an hour later. The doctor's orders were to soak my leg in hot water and massage the area.

That night I told my mother about the doctor's orders. As I've mentioned, my mother was a role model for me of strength and wisdom, especially in the face of a medical crisis. You may recall that she was born with undeveloped legs and wound up learning to walk on prostheses—without crutches. But there's more to that story: Early in her life—at only thirteen, *she* was the one who made the decision to have her deformed legs amputated . . . yes, both of them. So she knew a thing or two about legs, and she didn't like what she was hearing from me.

My mother also reminded me about my sister's thrombosis, and so she announced: "We're coming up there."

Early the next morning my parents left South Georgia for Atlanta. During their six-hour drive, my leg had swollen so much that I couldn't put any weight on it.

When they arrived, Mama took one look and said: "Get on the phone to that doctor. You have a blood clot."

We waited all day for his return call.

At noon the postman delivered a video of a program I had recently taped for public television. I popped the video into the VCR, then watched myself tell the story, "Why the 'Possum Has No Tail." It was to be the first and only time I ever saw myself tell a story on TV.

At 6:30 p.m., when the doctor still had not returned my call, Mama made the decision. "We're not waiting any longer. We're going to the Emergency Room."

Daddy rushed me to the small podiatry hospital where I'd had the elective surgery just five days earlier. It was surreal. That entire day seemed to move in slow motion, like it wasn't really happening. I didn't try to make sense of it.

My life was speeding out of my control like a runaway train.

6

Footprints

I glanced at the night sky as I dragged my left leg across the parking lot to the emergency room. It was a brilliant diamond-studded night, the kind that makes you sad because you know summer is fading. Little did I know that would be the last time I would gaze at the stars.

My father had his own way of taking charge. He scurried in ahead of me to get a wheelchair.

"Please don't fuss over me. I have been walking on it for two days. I can limp my way in."

Daddy ignored my plea.

All I had on my mind was Jerry at the lake, taking the boat out for one last spin. I wished I could be with him. I tried to ignore the fear creeping up in my belly. Not wanting to alarm my aging parents, I forced a smile and accepted the wheelchair. We entered the hospital at seven o'clock on September 2, 1987.

As we arrived, I thought of Diane, my new confidante and medical guru. I hoped she was on call that night. Diane had listened sympathetically as I confided my fears when we discussed my symptoms. I would be more comfortable in the ER with a registered nurse friend by my side.

Other thoughts flooded my mind. I had missed the last week of school in May because of the pernicious anemia. My family physician, who I'll call Dr. Right, assured me I was fine on my last visit in July. I had taken all the B12 treatments he'd prescribed. Yet the mysterious pain in my groin had continued to nag at me. Ideas of cancer had cluttered my brain . . . and my reasoning. I'd also grabbed a chance to satisfy a bit of vanity with what was supposed to have been liposuction, in addition to hernia repair.

And, truth be told now that I look back, I wanted to have my way, despite the wisdom and advice from Jerry, who I knew loved me despite his perhaps not-so-smooth communication skills.

I thought again of Dr. Right, who had been my family physician for six years. He knew me. He would have sent me to someone he trusted for a second opinion. Instead, I had listened to my new nurse friend and sought out an opinion from a stranger—Dr. Gucci Shoes.

Now I had a blood clot. Somewhere in my mind, I had a flash of the school bookkeeper grabbing my arm as I walked down the hall the day before surgery, "Don't go to that hospital. I've heard horror stories." What other signs had I ignored? What other desires had landed me on this runaway train?

The plastic surgeon arrived about fifteen minutes later. He examined the leg with a Doppler to measure the blood flow. He called in a vascular surgeon. Within an hour, a tall, lean older doctor arrived. He examined me and recommended immediate surgery.

I was scared. Things were moving too fast! The vascular surgeon was from another country. I knew that did not mean he wasn't capable, but his accent was so thick I couldn't understand his diagnosis. All I knew to do was call on my new friend, Nurse Diane, who personally knew these M.D.s, initials which I now thought stood for Medical Dummies.

Diane sounded surprised to hear from me. It wasn't like we were best friends and talked all the time. I told her the situation. "Diane, I'm scared. Tell me what to do."

"Your anesthetist is the most important consideration." She suggested one, but I learned he was not available. Then she hesitated. She had no other ideas. I asked her for another vascular surgeon, at least one with better English language skills. The vascular surgeon she suggested arrived at midnight, looking sharp and fresh—as if I could really tell his ability by his looks! He was wearing a crisp blue oxford shirt. He had coal black hair and dark eyes. I was in too much pain to notice his shoes.

After examining me he said, "Let's approach this more cautiously. Let's run some tests first."

I liked the sound of that! Reasonable.

Dr. Oxford Blue sent me to radiology for a venogram where the tech explained that the radiology dye they would inject could kill me if I was allergic to it.

"Why do you have to tell me that? I'm frightened enough!"

At two o'clock in the morning I was wheeled into the intensive care unit of the ER. Every fifteen minutes of that long night a nursing assistant took my blood pressure by placing the cuff over my injured leg and pumping away. I wanted to scream: "Wait a minute! Couldn't this cause the blood clot to move?" I never said a word.

It was a long night in Georgia as I watched the IV drip. I felt so alone and helpless. I hadn't seen my parents since my arrival. I wondered if Jerry knew where I was. He would come and take care of me. If cell phones had been available then, I would have called someone.

Early Friday morning, Jerry called. The nurse brought a phone to me so I could talk to him. Daddy had told him what was going on. He knew the leg had been swollen since he'd brought me home from the hospital on Sunday. He listened as I told him of the latest developments, then asked, "Should I leave work now and come over?"

I protested. "No, you'd just be spending the day in a waiting room." I heard myself assuring him, "My parents will be here."

Why do I put up a brave front when I want to shout that I'm scared?

I will always regret that I didn't see Jerry one last time before the surgery began.

That afternoon, a test had to be aborted because I had an adverse reaction to the medication that was supposed to calm me. Now they had me on a morphine drip.

At five, Dr. Oxford Blue consulted with my parents and me about the next step. He recommended surgery, because the femoral artery in my left leg was totally blocked from ankle to groin.

"What does that mean?" asked my dad.

"It appears there's a piece of the clot dangling by a thread. It's in danger of breaking off. It could be thrown into her lungs at any time. Your daughter could be at risk for pulmonary thrombosis."

I was terrified because I knew that could be fatal.

The doctor asked, "Do you want to have the surgery here or at St. Joseph's in Atlanta?" St. Joseph's was a prominent heart hospital thirty miles away.

"What's the risk in moving me?"

"Moving you could cause the clot to be thrown to your lungs."

By then, I was so out of it, I couldn't even remember his real name.

"Have you done this surgery here?"

"Yes, I've done it three times at this hospital. It's a simple procedure, and you will be awake. We will insert a Greenfield filter into your jugular vein." He touched my neck as he said this, leading me to believe the filter would rest there. "The procedure will take all of 45 minutes."

This was as clear to me as a morphine fog.

"How many times have you done this procedure in all?"

"Twenty-five times."

It never occurred to me to ask what could go wrong and what he would do if it did. I assumed that I understood well enough to make an informed decision. My parents were in shock and left the decision to me. Considering how dangerous it would be to move me, I opted for surgery at that hospital. In retrospect, I was making life-changing decisions under the influence of large amounts of morphine. Not good . . . a little knowledge is a dangerous thing.

The doctor failed to clarify an important piece of information: The 32-inch long instrument launching the filter into my vascular system would be threaded through my heart to get to my groin. If I had known that, I'm sure I would have insisted on consulting a cardiologist about complications. The filter's function was not to capture the clot in my leg and move it to my neck for removal. Instead the filter (imagine a badminton birdie with six fishhooks) was designed to anchor itself into my vena cava wall and break up the clot, eliminating the danger. Had I known the extent of this invasive procedure, my decision might have been different.

Also, no one made me aware that small hospitals like this one sometimes did not have the proper equipment in case of an emergency. In 1987, there were only three hospitals in metro Atlanta with heart-lung machines. This was not one of them.

Later I would learn that any time your attending physician calls in a specialist, your physician should be present to help you make informed decisions. Dr. Gucci Shoes was in the hospital but not present for the consultation.

My mother, father, and I sat stunned, trying to absorb all this. I could only hope I was making the right decision. A nurse reassured me that the hospital had a new image—not to worry. Apparently she was aware of the hospital's reputation.

They prepared me for immediate surgery, but Jerry did not arrive until after I had been taken to the operating room.

Lying on the surgical table, I listened to the preparations. They placed blinders over my eyes. I relaxed knowing my nurse friend, Diane, was by the doctor's side.

After the surgery began, I heard him ask in a strained voice, "Get me a . . . " and then he named a certain surgical instrument that today I don't recall.

What I do remember was recognizing Diane's alarmed voice. "We don't have that, doctor."

I'm sure I fidgeted. *What? How can a surgical center not have the instruments they need!*

He asked for something else, and Diane again replied in the negative.

I wanted to jump up and yell, "What do you mean—you don't have it?"

Then he asked for a stainless steel wire.

How strange!

All this time I was in and out of consciousness. I tried to reason. *I'm in an operating room—it's going to be okay. If I were on a battlefield, I might not be so safe.*

But the fact is this: At that moment, I was in a battle for my life.

Remember that stainless steel wire? When the filter was dispatched, it misfired and began floating around in my heart. Rather than stopping to explain to the surgical team why the procedure was aborted, the doctor was attempting to pull out the filter using the wire he requested.

And that wasn't all. To see what he was doing, the doctor would switch on a fluoroscope, a radiation tool he could use only for moments at a time to see his progress—how far he'd been able to move the filter since his last look. So after taking another quick peek, he would turn it off again and try once more to fish out the filter. He was doing this over and over, not only exposing me to radiation but doing this dangerous procedure in the dark. And inside my heart, no less!

Of course, I would learn all this later, including the devastating result: His instrument had snagged the largest vein of my heart called the vena cava, causing a tiny tear near my heart valve.

I was bleeding out.

My life was passing before me. I envisioned the large black and white clock that hangs above the chalkboard in every classroom in America. I saw faces of children I had taught over the years. Many of these were students who had made an imprint on my soul, struggling with their self-esteem, learning disabilities, or behavioral issues.

I began praying. As I did, words from my favorite poem, "Footprints in the Sand," rang in my head. You may be familiar with this poem. The author, while encountering the Lord, expresses gratitude that He always walked alongside. Then the author questions the Lord, asking why, when he needed Him the most, only one set of footprints was visible in the sand. The Lord assures the author He was there when he needed Him—carrying him.

The words I recounted may not have been exact, but my Lord was listening as I prayed for Him to carry me. I knew He would.

Suddenly, a vision of Daddy flashed before my eyes. He was lifting me up, showing me how to chin myself on the chinning bar in our yard when I was a little girl. I knew he was there to catch me, but I held on desperately, afraid of falling. I felt the same danger in that tiny hospital as I held on for dear life. *Dear Heavenly Father, please give me a second chance. I have so much left to do in this life. There's the fellowship and so many lives I want to touch. I don't want it to end here. I want to live.*

At that exact moment I tried to sit up on the operating table. The drape covering my body fell to the floor, revealing what the vascular surgeon already knew. Diane gasped. "She's cyanotic!" As a nurse, Diane realized I was experiencing oxygen deprivation.

The next thing I remember was the doctor asking, "Has anyone told her parents?"

I wanted to shout: "Wait! Told my parents what? Am I dead?"

I felt a rush and that must have been when the hemorrhaging was getting worse. I prayed as my heart slowly deflated. *I'm in your hands, Lord. I can't hold on any longer.* I then let go, and God carried me.

At one point someone went to discuss the options with my parents. It was Friday night of Labor Day weekend, and the traffic was at a crawl across the city. Thank God, Daddy had the good sense to say, "Don't send her to another hospital in an ambulance. Call Life Flight!"

And they did. Thank you, Daddy, for being so on top of things. He helped to save my life.

I vaguely remembered the whirring helicopter, and Jerry running beside me on the gurney calling out, "I love you!"

The next thing I knew, I woke up unable to see.

7

Blind as a Bat

As I regained consciousness in the Cardiac Care Unit I was terrified, because I couldn't seem to open my eyes, and I didn't understand why. I didn't realize my eyes were open; I just couldn't see.

My sister Sandra had just arrived from Blackshear, Georgia. Jerry took Sandra's hand and led her into my room explaining, "You're not going to recognize Fiona—just be prepared."

Sandra gasped. "That's not my sister!"

I looked like I had been hooked up to a helium tank and blown up. The blood from hemorrhaging had settled in my arms, neck, and head.

Sandra told me much later that I looked like the Coneheads from *Saturday Night Live*. "You had no neck! The top of your head was narrow, then it widened out to your shoulders. It was so grotesque. You were unrecognizable."

When Sandra found out that I hadn't told my friends about the surgery, she called them all. My closest friend, Marie, dropped everything to rush to my side. She, too, was shocked at the sight of me propped up and puffed up like the Pillsbury doughboy. Tubes were streaming from every orifice in my body. She squeezed my hand and whispered, "You wouldn't have made a pretty fat woman, girlfriend." We had known each other since we were nineteen. As we both grew into womanhood, I aspired to be the nurturing, charming, and talented mother I watched her become as she raised her three children. Marie stayed in the hospital for two days and cared for me as my Florence Nightingale.

I couldn't breathe on my own. The tubes were my lifeline, but they hindered my ability to communicate with anyone. I tried to talk with the tube in my mouth. I wanted desperately to tell them I couldn't see. No one understood. Worried that I had no lesson plans ready for my students, I wanted someone to call the school to let them know I wouldn't return on Monday as planned. I anxiously tried to draw words on my sister's palm. I wrote for Sandra not to send flowers, but instead to purchase books for the school library. She let out a sob. She thought I was planning my funeral. I don't know what I was thinking. We were all in shock.

To make matters worse, my period came unexpectedly with a flow so heavy I was on the verge of hemorrhaging again. They sent someone to the women's hospital across the street for maternity pads to manage the excessive bleeding. These pads were so large I could have worn them as a bandana. No one offered me a sanitary belt to hold them on, and my family kept forgetting to bring my underwear. Whenever someone assisted me to the bathroom, the pad fell to the floor. Forget about dignity! There was none. The shock of waking up blind kept me from thinking about embarrassing moments.

After a couple of days I was moved to a private room where I was alone during the mornings. St. Joseph's was a Catholic hospital. Many nuns visited my room, but no one seemed to know what to say. The medical staff didn't talk to me or give me any tips about living with this darkness. They seemed to ignore the fact that I couldn't see. Apparently the nuns didn't know how to give me guidance to help me move on and off the gurney each time I was taken to the lab for CT scans. They didn't explain why they weren't doing anything about what I assumed was my temporary loss of vision or what the treatment plan was. I don't think they talked to anyone in my family for several days. The doctors just kept coming in and examining my eyes and saying, "Hmmm. You can't see anything?" I imagined they looked like the Three Stooges wearing white coats and stethoscopes.

"That's right," I replied.

Many unanswered questions would hang in the balance for three more years.

However, by the time doctors were trying to diagnose my lack of vision, I was learning bits and pieces of important information. For one, the fact that I was alive was a miracle. I had flat-lined once during the flight between hospitals. Fortunately, they had equipment on board to keep me alive. By the way, Daddy's insistence that I be air-lifted was insightful for a reason other than the danger of transporting me by ground. Seems the doctor who was basically trying to fish an object he'd lost out of my heart had nurses phoning other hospitals, begging for help. No doctor would commit because they knew they couldn't get across the city. It was Friday evening of a holiday weekend during rush hour traffic.

I also learned that, after I arrived at St. Joseph's hospital, several friends and family members gathered to keep vigil in the waiting room. They had been informed that my condition was critical, that my odds for survival were slim, at best. Several tender stories resulted from their time spent supporting me in this caring way. For example, my niece, Paige, called my friend, Cathy, whom I had not spoken to in nearly a year. She had been my son's babysitter ever since he was six months old. Cathy and I were so close for thirteen years, but a disagreement had kept us apart. She rushed to the hospital and was there by the time I got out of surgery.

Cathy was the one who called my ex-husband and handed the phone to our son Chance. He and Chance wept together over the phone.

Poor Jerry was having a different sort of experience. He'd been told by his best friend and a relative that it was a mistake for me to be in the hospital where the surgery went so wrong. But since we weren't married, he had no authority to have me moved. He'd spent hours trying to find another doctor who would review my case. By the time I was moved to St. Joseph's, he was so discouraged and exhausted that he spent most of his time in the waiting room with the others, slumped with his head in his hands, staring at the floor.

After the A-Team of heart specialists repaired my heart, which was my third surgery in less than a week, my parents felt that the crisis had passed, and they returned to my house, exhausted. My son held my strong, capable mother as she cried—something we had rarely seen before.

I met with the cardiologist who headed the A-Team weeks later in his office. I told him, "God saved my life."

He jokingly replied, "Me and God!"

He was a kind and brilliant man. I know God gave him miracle hands, and I began to think of him as Dr. Miracle Worker.

After a week of the parade of doctors trying to figure out what happened, the vascular surgeon gave us the diagnosis—hysterical blindness due to trauma. He told me the consensus was that once the shock wore off, I should recover my eyesight. However, there were no guarantees.

Due to the severity of the blood clot I had to be on Coumadin. The blood thinner required a strict diet with no roughage such as salads, because the combination could cause bleeding. My instructions were to call my doctor if I had a fever over 100. This only added to my fear.

I was fitted for expensive surgical stockings. *Surely I won't get a run in these.* It took a team of horses to pull them on. I joked that I would prefer a team of construction workers.

During the next two weeks while I was alone in my hospital bed, I mentally tried to lift the scales from my eyes. I saw Daddy, but I knew it wasn't real because in my mind's eye he looked the way he did when I was a little girl. I also thought I saw my grandmother Graham—who had been dead for three years. Then I recalled that she was visually impaired from macular degeneration. I remembered Nellie, a neighbor from my childhood, who was also blind. My memories seemed to establish a disturbing pattern. Would I be blind for the rest of my life? Being in shock is like living in a dream—you know life is moving along, but there's no sense of reality.

The highlight of each day was Jerry's visit. He came around one o'clock to feed me. One day he was late. When he saw the food tray, untouched and placed near the foot of my bed, he asked, "Didn't you get fed?"

"No, is my food here?"

The food handlers, unaware that I was blind, had set down the tray quietly without speaking. He later had a sign placed over my bed telling hospital staff that I was blind.

I was reminded several times how lucky I was that the A-team had been on call September 3 when I was life-flighted to St. Joseph's hospital. They were my knights in shining armor. These surgeons had saved my life. The captain of this amazing team, the remarkable cardiologist I now regarded as Dr. Miracle Worker, had taken a portion of the pericardium, which is the lining of the heart, to patch the tear of my superior vena cava.

I needed heart rehabilitation. The next several days of recovery were spent teaching me to strengthen my heart. Losing seven pints of blood in emergency surgery left my heart muscle so weak that I would have to do a lot of walking. Breathing on my own and regaining use of my arms were the first steps. I still had seven pints of blood lodged in my tissues that had to dissipate somewhere . . . somehow. There was no question that this recovery would take many, many months. I wasn't clear-headed enough to ask anything. My prognosis wasn't discussed with me.

The neurologist from my A-team was gentle. I asked no questions . . . he offered no answers. I didn't know what to ask. He would be the one to break the news in a later visit.

On the last day of my hospital stay, the nurse helped me get dressed to go home. While my son was bringing the car around she pulled the pink blouse over my head, but it wouldn't button at the neck. The reality of my swollen body sunk in. Tears streamed down my face. I couldn't even look in the mirror to see how awful I looked! The nurse brought me downstairs to meet my son. I don't even remember what we said.

The nurse guided me into the low-slung Camaro. I could feel the warm September air kiss my face. It seemed to pick me up and set me down in the car. My mind raced. It was Jerry's birthday. I couldn't even shop for a present or card. Anxiety crept in. What were the doctor's orders? I could not think. I rested my head against the car window and felt the tears dripping from my eyes. I turned away, hoping my nineteen-year-old son would not notice. He tried valiantly to cheer me up by describing the flowers along the highway. He couldn't know the despair I felt hearing about images I feared one day might be gone forever from my mind.

A few weeks later I was in my neurologist's office. The kind doctor stooped to tie my shoes and gently answered my obvious question, "When will I see again?" They had given me hope when I left the hospital.

"The good news is that you are a walking miracle. You had a team of brilliant surgeons who patched you up."

I quipped, "Like Humpty Dumpty, I've been put back together again!"

Then silence for a moment as he gathered his thoughts.

"My dear, you probably are not going to regain your sight. It's possible the optic nerve could regenerate itself . . . but doubtful."

It must have been very hard for him to say those words.

An MRI had told the tale. The cyanosis I had experienced, or oxygen deprivation, basically destroyed my optic nerve. But the result could have been so much worse. When a patient is cyanotic, the blood pools around the vital organs for survival, leaving others to fend for themselves which means that some parts of the body may suffer severe damage. The first area to lose oxygen in my case was the optic nerve. Doctors have told me this is highly unusual—by all accounts, I should have been comatose rather than simply losing my vision.

It's another lesson in how the body is a fantastic machine. In drastic hemorrhaging, such as what happened to me, the little blood soldiers run to the rescue. They stand guard at the vital organs until the bleeding is under control or death occurs. So many were needed to protect organs such as my lungs. And, although they weren't able to guard my optic nerve, located in the head, I've been grateful for the work of these little blood soldiers during the precious moments when I could have suffered brain damage.

I didn't comprehend all this during my visit to the neurologist that day. I don't know why Humpty Dumpty came to my mind; maybe it's because I'm a storyteller. In fact, I was in such shock after what he said that the question flashed in my mind: Did Humpty Dumpty have trouble navigating his steps, cutting his food, finding his clothes . . . or did he even bother? I was faced with that reality. How easily depression can crowd its way in, even temporarily! In my case, I had a mother who taught me to face adversity with a sense of humor. I had the added benefit of friends and family members to lift my spirits.

On the way home from the doctor's office Cathy and I stopped for lunch. I met Cathy back when she was in my fourth grade class. She was a wide-eyed blonde whom I felt like I helped to raise. I am as proud of her witty personality as if I were her mother. Trying to cheer me up she said, "Let's look around in Macy's." I really wasn't in the mood, but Cathy was a friend who could always make me laugh. Walking wasn't easy. We giggled over how often we used the words "look," "see," and "watch out." We stumbled along—neither of us knew anything about sighted guides and how they eventually would become a part of my life.

Suddenly Cathy thundered, "Blind as a bat!" She tried to get me to laugh to keep us both from crying as we maneuvered the public restroom. Quite naturally she led me to the handicap stall. I discovered I did not like having so much space to feel my way around. And the toilet seat—yuck! *How am I going to do this?*

What cracked us up the most was when I waddled out of the restroom asking, "Cathy, what's restricting my walk? Something feels strange. What is it?" Cathy laughed so hard that I could hardly understand her response.

She maneuvered our quick U-turn back into the restroom and blurted out, "You forgot to pull up your underwear!" I was so out of touch with my own body that I couldn't even remember *that.*

My world was definitely upside down. I struggled each day to survive through the frustration. Like a bird with its wings clipped, I felt paralyzed. Eventually I would learn to hone in on other senses, much like a bat.

My family and friends were suffering along with me. They often cajoled, "Don't be impatient."

"You're pushy!"

"Could you be a little less demanding?"

They did not say these things in a mean way but out of their own frustration. Marie told me later that they always waited until I left the room before they cried. Maybe I'm glad I couldn't see the grief on their faces. My blindness had created a communication gap. I had no visual trigger to sense their emotions. They had no point of reference for understanding the prison that darkness had created.

The first time my sister took me for a walk, she guided me too close to a sign on a pole, and I scraped my head. She said, "Don't cry about the bump on your head, Fiona. Things could be so much worse. You could be six feet under." We laughed over this . . . comic relief, I guess. I'm sure she was crying on the inside.

I can't imagine how many times Jerry fell apart when he looked around at how I had decorated my townhouse, remembering how much I had enjoyed it. Years later he told me he cried each time he took a shower as he thought of things I couldn't do or see.

All I could think about was never seeing the sunrise, the faces of my future grandchildren, or my son as a man. I became frozen in time, left with the memories of the way we all looked when I was forty-four.

Several weeks later I met with the heart surgeon. I asked if he thought the patch would hold and shared my fears that one day the repair would split or wear out. His dry reply didn't give me a lot of reassurance. "I don't know. This was the first time I'd ever done this." At the time I didn't know if he was joking or serious.

He had no idea the impact that statement would have. Over the next year, I had several panic attacks that sent me rushing to the doctor. I was convinced my heart would burst. That's how they described my grandmother's death, "her heart burst," which I believe was the way they described heart attacks many years ago. I went through a year of anxiety attacks, thinking I was going to die whenever I was under stress. In my mind a fever meant internal bleeding. I worried about the strength of the patch, not aware that scar tissue actually makes it stronger.

Six months after losing my eyesight, I sat before my family doctor and explained that I didn't know why I had such a tough time getting out of bed each day. I wondered if I'd developed anemia again, a condition that had plagued me often in my life.

"Fiona," said Dr. Right. "You can't see the forest for the trees! You're depressed. You are an independent woman in a dependent body—screaming to get out!" I scoffed at the idea. He went on to say he believed in me and thought I would write a book someday, dedicated to Christa McAuliffe.

I didn't appreciate the wisdom of this statement at the time, but looking back I understand. Every time I was feeling down, God put someone in my path to redirect me, encourage me, or make me smile. Amazing!

8

Friends in My Path

If it had not been for Elayne, my social worker friend, I would not have known the next step after my two-week hospital stay. We'd met nine years earlier on a trip to Paris. We were both bumped from one flight to another and sat in adjacent seats chatting happily about our tour of France. She was a cute thirty-two-year-old single blonde, and I was three years older, a married teacher away from home for the first time. Like me, she was a take-charge woman. She came to my house to whip me into shape. When she arrived, I was not sure what to do next and glad for her take-charge personality.

The project for my Christa McAuliffe Fellowship had to be completed in one year. I would face losing it if I didn't start mobility training immediately. Storytelling gigs that had been lined up before I lost my sight were already on my calendar for later in the fall. I was determined not to cancel them. Plus, the members of Southern Order of Storytellers (SOS) refused to accept my resignation as President. They even re-elected me for the next year.

On Elayne's first visit to my house she asked what happened to my hair. I told her I was way overdue for new color—my roots were surely dark—so I'd found a bottle of Clairol and attempted a touch-up. I figured it was a little tricky for a blind person to do this, but it was better than dark roots.

"Only you, Fiona, would try that. It's a disaster, girlfriend. We've got to do it again." That's what I mean about Elayne taking charge.

After re-doing my hair, she called her friend in a county vocational rehab office. By coincidence, he was someone who had sung with me in the choir at Kelly's Chapel Methodist Church ten years earlier. Fred took charge by arranging for a counselor to come to my home. Just think! If Elayne and I hadn't been bumped from that flight, I might never have had these resources.

The irony was that earlier in the year I had visited this same rehabilitation office as a speaker, and now I required their training as a client. Here's a quick flash-forward for your amusement . . .

The following spring I was booked to give the keynote address at the Helen Keller Foundation Conference. I decided to speak about my first in-home rehab experience. The story went something like this:

Unaware I was my instructor's first client, I was a bit unruly. She was teaching me how to protect myself as I made my way around the house without sight. For example, she told me to use my knuckles to follow the walls so I wouldn't injure my fingers when I came to a corner. She also instructed me how to position my hands as protection for certain parts of my body, in case I ran into furniture when I moved away from the walls.

But I was mischievous and couldn't resist making a joke when she told me: "Put your right hand in front of your chest and your left in front of your groin area."

I piped up, "My growin' area? What's that?" Her southern drawl was thicker than mine. She was not amused.

I continued to share how she tried to teach me the way a blind person should pour milk, and I blurted out, "I don't like milk!"

She made me sew tiny Braille tags onto my socks. I protested: "Do I have to?"

"If you want to know the color of your socks, you do." She was serious.

I was trying to laugh to hide my pain.

At the end of my speech, a woman stood up and identified herself as that very rehab instructor. She was a good sport. So much for making fun of the teacher behind her back!

When it came time to decide where I would go for mobility training, I was presented with two choices: Center for the Visually Impaired (CVI) in Atlanta or the Roosevelt Warm Springs Institute for Rehabilitation in Warm Springs, Georgia. After the interview at CVI, I called Warm Springs and spoke to the director. He described what a year of living in the dormitory would be like . . . how I would learn to navigate stairs, halls, bathrooms, etc. I shrank in fear. Could I do this? Staying at Warm Springs sounded very isolating.

I pictured being in a strange place, having to find my way down the hall to a toilet and shower. I had so many conveniences at home, and I was beginning to learn my way around my townhouse by feel. I was intrigued at how I could visualize my furniture. I wondered if I would always conjure up those vivid images. Would I forget what blue, red, and mauve look like? I could "see" the mauve wallpaper I had put in the kitchen and bath just the year before. I knew my clothes. I felt safe there.

Weighing my choices of Warm Springs in South Georgia or the Center for the Visually Impaired right in Atlanta, I realized what a frightening prospect it would be to leave my friends and family. Did I really want the challenge of a new environment for a year? Would I still have a boyfriend when I came home?

I concluded that the Center for the Visually Impaired was a better option for me. Thanks to my friends, Elayne and Margaret Ann, I was accepted at CVI right away. Elayne had worked with their director.

Margaret Ann and I had become friends when she supported me as the president of SOS. She had gone to college with the President of the Georgia Academy for the Blind, located in Macon. He helped her to get me accepted, because I had a fellowship and needed priority training. Yet another obstacle loomed: CVI had a waiting list. I could hardly believe all three of them pulled strings to get me in. My friends got me on the right track and accepted for training at CVI.

When I got there, the counselor at CVI explained, "We typically discourage people from seeking training too soon after their loss."

Grief of any kind, including loss of eyesight, can last one to four years. But they had made an exception because of my fellowship, and less than four months from the day I woke up blind, I was enrolled in mobility training, Braille, and cooking.

I still faced the challenge of how to get there each day. CVI was twenty-five miles away. My boyfriend worked in the other direction. I couldn't think of anyone who could help.

Just in time, Bob happened to call to invite me to speak at his Kiwanis Club. I had met Bob after doing a mime storytelling gig earlier that year. We had chatted and I'd given him my card. Six months later he read about my fellowship and thought it would be an interesting topic for his Kiwanis Club.

I rushed to answer the phone, and drew in a breath when I realized it was someone I knew from before the surgery. "Well, something has changed since we met—I am blind." (It was still hard to say the dreadful word.)

Bob didn't hesitate. "Don't worry about that. I had a roommate in college who was blind. I will pick you up and be a helpful guide." I said yes.

Although I had other gigs lined up for later, I was bubbling over with the news of my first speaking engagement since going blind. At the same time I was tormented with fears and doubts. Put yourself in my place. I'd been invited to speak on a topic that thrilled me—my Christa McAuliffe Fellowship to teach storytelling. Bob's Kiwanis Club would be a perfect audience. But would I fit in? Would they see past my blindness to hear my message? Would their interest and applause be for the cause of storytelling and the opportunity I was given or would it be motivated by curiosity and pity for my sudden loss of eyesight?

So many things could go wrong. Remember that Bob's telephone call came after I had been blind for about a month. I didn't have training yet on how to instruct sighted people to help me. I didn't even have a cane. I was at a point in my grief over the loss of my sight and the acceptance of its challenges where I was actually embarrassed about my blindness. I felt like I wasn't a whole person, and yet I'd made the choice to be public about my condition by accepting speaking opportunities. Although I didn't analyze it this closely at the time, looking back I wonder: Was I operating from courage or ignorance? What a jumble of circumstances and emotions! For example, gaining a perspective of space as I entered the room where the Kiwanis Club met would take time, perhaps years. Would I be wobbly? Would I appear pathetic? I so desperately wanted to fit in with those people—able-bodied folks like I'd been only a few weeks earlier.

Over time, of course, I came to grips with the reality that all people are imperfect in different ways and all have fears at some level. Yet back then I already knew that blindness is a horrifying condition for most people. The fear of blindness in many adults dates back to their fear of the dark during childhood. Some people—deep in their subconscious—recoil from having contact with blind people, thinking: What if she bumps into something? What if the condition is somehow contagious? Of course, that last one is strictly a fear they can't articulate but it exists all the same, because being in the presence of a blind person is a reminder of how fragile their own vision must be, how a surgery could go wrong for them also.

The bottom line was this: Would my blindness be a distraction to this influential group? Would it negate the message of opportunity I would be presenting for school children to accelerate their learning through the storytelling technique? Would the Kiwanis Club members be watching for me to blunder instead of hearing my joy about receiving the fellowship, travelling throughout my home state, and teaching these valuable skills? How desperately I wanted to rise to the occasion, to demonstrate my competence, and to live up to the professional ideals of the fellowship I'd been awarded.

Bob's phone call began my long journey to acceptance of my condition and to wholeness as a person who considers herself blind yet having vision. I mentioned this in Chapter One, "My Nightlife Is 24/7." Here are a few truths that journey taught me over the years . . .

As horrible as the experience has been in so many ways, I know God allowed me to go blind. Yet He has been with me every step of the way, from the operating room to the moment I am writing this very sentence to you, my reader. Because of my blindness, I have sought His guidance in a deeper way than I did when I was on a sighted path. I don't claim to know if this was God's reason. All I can say is what I've experienced.

Another lesson I've learned in a more profound way is that faith requires an attitude of submission. It should be obvious to you by now that I am strong-willed and that submitting to even the advice and opinions of others can be a stretch for me. Am I still stubborn? Yes. But now I work harder at accepting help, even seeking it. This chapter on "Friends in My Path" only scratches the surface of all the people who came into my life when I needed them or who stayed by my side when they could have drifted away.

I said I'm not a preacher. But I'll share a scripture that has particular meaning to me and may to you. It's from Luke 12:48: "... *everyone who has been given much, much will be demanded; and from the one who has been entrusted with much, much more will be asked.*" Writing this book is hard—and, frankly, expensive—for a blind person to accomplish. But I believe it's an act of submission and obedience so I can tell you my experiences and, from those, your life will be enriched. For example, I hope you are learning the realities, good and bad, of my becoming blind. Think of this: I came very close to dying on the operating table, but God allowed me to live. Also, no matter what might be our problems—and we all have them—we can learn coping mechanisms. In addition, I've learned that God is with us and He puts people in our path to help.

As my story continues, I hope you'll see how I was in a sort of darkness before I became blind yet now that I live in literal darkness I can see truths I never knew. I have greater vision for my journey. It's what people of faith call seeing the Light with a capital "L."

Ironically, the Christa McAuliffe Fellowship was a lifeline. It made me reach. And the timing was perfect.

Well, back to the Kiwanis Club where Bob turned out to be a perfect gentleman. He set me at ease until I realized when the food came that I could not cut up my salad or the steak. I turned to Bob, calling on my inner Southern Belle and batting my eyelashes, and said, "I don't know you intimately, but would you please cut up my food?"

He chuckled and complied. On the way home from Kiwanis, he asked a lot of questions about my plans. I told him I could not start my Georgia speaking tour until I had figured out how to get to CVI for rehab. "The glitch is that the place is twenty-five miles from my house. I don't know anyone who isn't working."

Bob called me a week later with a plan. He had asked members of his Kiwanis Club and their spouses to take turns driving me back and forth to school for as long as it took. The club presented me with a Braille watch at the next meeting so I could be on time for my rides. Bob and his friends were faithful, kind people whom I came to know and love. I thought my repayment for their kindness should be entertaining them with stories and wearing a broad smile each day. They never knew how scared I was while exiting their car, carefully tapping with my new cane to find the door of CVI.

Friends come and go in our lives. Bob was there for a reason and a season. I will be indebted forever.

I attended the Center for the Visually Impaired for two and a half months. The recommended coursework was for one year. No, I didn't master Braille. Nor did I master mobility—practicing with a cane each day on Peachtree Street was tedious. I was not a good student. I was the kind of student who tried to coax her instructor to stop for coffee and a chat. I just wanted to be done with learning and get on with life.

9

They Say

The official Christa McAuliffe Fellowship certificate arrived in the mail just weeks after I returned home from the hospital. I eagerly tore open the package. As I pretended to feel the words, I found the national seal. My fingers traced it gingerly. It was so impressive. I stood there, wiping away the tears. My emotions were a mix of sadness and pride. I thought again about that fateful day, January 28, 1986, when Christa McAuliffe and all those astronauts died aboard the Space Shuttle *Challenger*. Because of that tragedy, I had this award. In the blink of an eye, so much had changed. One thing that remained the same, though, was my drive to forge ahead.

They say, "It takes years to get over life-changing events." I didn't have the luxury of time to recover from the trauma of waking up blind from surgery. I had to learn to cope—there was no other choice. I had to learn to dress, do makeup and hair, cut my food, and even eat. If I was to communicate in the sighted world, I also had to learn to use a computer. But now, just dialing a telephone stressed me. I cried over trying to operate a tape recorder or put in new batteries. There was so much to relearn . . . I couldn't even imagine what my future would hold.

Little did I know this was just the beginning of my trials.

I should explain that, when I became blind, no meaningful legislative protection existed for people with disabilities—another word I had a hard time saying. The Americans with Disabilities Act was signed into law by President George H. W. Bush in 1990. Known as the ADA, it has been amended over the years, most recently during the administration of the younger President Bush. The ADA is a complex body of law which I won't attempt to explain, although I'm grateful it exists. It was needed, not only to deal legally with issues affecting disabled people, but to promote a higher level of understanding.

As you read this chapter, please understand that I am not complaining. I am only trying to give you a glimpse into my new normal a few weeks after losing my eyesight. I feel that I would not be doing the story justice if I left out the situations I describe, and I promised to be open and candid in this book. However, please understand that I cannot say for sure whether each situation would have been handled differently if the Americans with Disabilities Act had already become established law. It is my understanding that benefits resulting from the ADA are decided on a case-by-case basis.

Due to some quirky rule, my leased automobile was repossessed. The teachers' group insurance policy would not allow any driver to be insured other than the teacher. They notified the leasing company of the cancellation of my policy, and my car was towed away in the middle of the night. I felt like a criminal as though I had done the dastardly deed of making myself blind.

Several years later I settled with the leasing agency. That pretty blue Chrysler LeBaron I drove for eighteen months could have cost me another $10,000, the amount I still owed, if I had not made a new friend who offered to help me negotiate with the leasing company. They accepted a final settlement amount which was within my means.

I had no idea that the lease agreement or the amount due were negotiable. As they say, some things are learned the hard way.

Yes, there were days when I considered staying in bed and wrapping myself in my comforter, but I knew that would bring me no *real* comfort.

A month after losing my car, the benefits department of the Gwinnett County school district contacted me with a second dilemma. A clause in the contract stipulated that I must return to my classroom upon completion of the fellowship duties or else I had to return the grant money. At this point, I didn't know if I would be given my old job back since I could no longer see. The questions overwhelmed me. Would I have to return the certificate, declining the fellowship? What would the U.S. Department of Education do if I was in violation of the terms? Would I have to return the money? Would they make an exception for me?

I called my Congressman, Lindsay Thomas, whom I had known while growing up in South Georgia. Lindsay listened sympathetically to my plight. He told me there were others who had valid reasons for not being able to return to the same classroom the next year. He and a colleague submitted a bill to Congress to change this specific regulation. I am grateful that the terms of my contract were rewritten. My grant was intact. Thank you, Lindsay, for taking this on.

• • •

I faced a third obstacle when I learned I was in danger of losing my disability insurance. The benefits director called to notify me that the grant money recently wired to my personal account would be reported to the IRS as income, even though the money was earmarked for my training and travel expenses for the speaking tour. It was a Catch-22. If I accepted the grant, I would forfeit my short-term disability benefits, which were scheduled to begin soon.

Let's see now—earlier I'd had the problem with my mortgage payments and now I'd gone through repossession of my automobile. I was experiencing the crisis of *possibly* losing my job, and now my employer was telling me this most prestigious honor could cause me to lose my benefits. What next?

As I lay in bed on a chilly December morning with the phone to my ear, I listened to the benefits director suggest that I might want to decline the fellowship. *Decline it?* How could I decline my incentive to live?

I slammed down the phone and cried whale-like tears. How could they do this to me? *This is just cruel.* The first installment already had been wired to my checking account—three thousand bucks that was like a hot plate. *Should I touch it?*

I knew I had to keep careful records. None of these funds could be used for personal expenses such as mortgage payments. Budgeting for a driver was easy enough, but who would keep the records, write the checks, and help me with bookings? I was trying to learn how to walk, eat, and dress. Could I accomplish anything more?

I dug in and began looking for a driver. Tracey had been one of the teens in my church when my son was little. We had been close since she was nine, but I'd lost touch with her after she married. I called to see if she could work for me. She had recently finished a degree in psychology but hadn't started working yet. She agreed. I had my driver!

Next, I was determined to feel out my employer about my job. My friend Marie was spending the week with me. We discussed what I must do. Although my body was still weak and swollen, I called Dr. Crews, superintendent of Gwinnett County schools, and made an appointment. While we were on the phone, I reminded him of the positive PR this award could bring to the county. I was Georgia's first recipient of the Christa McAuliffe Fellowship—that had to count for something! Could they risk allowing this honor to turn sour? His response would tell me if anyone thought I could complete the tasks ahead. We agreed to meet October 1.

Marie drove me to meet with the superintendent. As we walked into the building, I turned to her and smiled. "Don't worry, I'm wearing my good luck dress." That jade and white rayon two-piece dress served me well the day I was awarded American History Teacher of the Year by the Daughters of the American Revolution (DAR). The previous year I had been first runner-up for Teacher of the Year at Duluth Middle School. I had been told I was a good teacher—no, a great teacher—by my school principals. These awards, records of accomplishment, and words of praise by principals were in my personnel file. My hope was that the school superintendent would not want to lose me.

In preparing for our meeting, I'm sure Dr. Crews was thinking about the liability of having a blind teacher in an eighth grade classroom. Returning to work would require assistance. I would need an aide. No doubt he thought of the expense for the county. But all I wanted was my job back. Having been blind for less than three months, I dreamed of walking to school with my new guide dog in tow. I had no idea how long it took to get such a dog, and I certainly didn't know how much adjustment was involved or how long it would take. As I stepped into his office, I thought of my priorities. I was afraid of losing my livelihood, but keeping the grant had to be my primary focus.

Trying to display confidence, I reached out to shake my boss's hand. He found it, and—following a warm greeting—I reminded him of the time he had called me for assistance with a speech. He was looking for a Brer Rabbit story about being resourceful. (At the time, I was surprised that he knew I was the storytelling teacher for his school system.) We chuckled, then I jumped right in to discuss going back to work. I was prepared for some confrontation, but he offered none. Instead he was kind, diplomatic, and, no doubt, sensitive to a teacher who had just lost her sight and now had to deal with losing her career. He knew he wasn't going to offer me my job back, nor was he planning to offer me another position, but he could tell my jaw was set.

I don't think Dr. Crews had the heart to tell me I would be too much of a liability in an eighth grade classroom, so he urged me to take my return to work slowly. He probably knew better than me how much work I was facing to rehabilitate. He commented that he admired my courage for coming to see him. He promised that he would look into the matter of my disability payments. I never heard from him again on the matter.

After our meeting, I had no idea what lay ahead. I went before the benefits board to plead my case several times. Friends mentioned that I could apply for graduate school to begin earning a Ph.D., but I couldn't imagine learning to listen to a textbook and I didn't want to take on more education.

Two long years would pass before I knew for sure that they would allow me to keep the benefits package. I never knew what part the superintendent played in keeping my benefits intact, but I was ever grateful that they decided not to make an issue of it. Finally, someone unofficially told me they would not bother me again.

They say, "Never burn your bridges." I believe that's a wise statement. Several years later, Dr. Crews had taken a position with the Southeastern Regional Education Board (SREB) and contacted me about doing a storytelling program for educators. He suggested that I submit a proposal to the board. His respect for my work really boosted my confidence.

My resolve to hold onto the fellowship paralleled my mother's determination to remain in her childhood home in 1944. After her father died, her lawyer explained that without a last will and testament, she must bid for her home like any other person at the auction. "Just come to the courthouse steps and make the first bid."

She did. Standing on those steps on her two artificial legs and looking into the eyes of the crowd, Mama pled, "Most of you know me. I have lived at 816 Highway Avenue since I was five years old. I took care of both of my parents there until their deaths. I would like to make the first bid." No one bid against her.

Owning a home was the most precious asset most people had in the '40s. Now in the '80s, I felt that my job or ability to make a living was my only asset. My mother and I both stood bravely, for the same reasons.

They say, "Never give up."

For a brief moment I became my mother that October day in 1987, asking for my job in Dr. Crews' office and vowing never to give up the fellowship.

10

Braille Fail

In my sighted life, as a young teacher I believed people in my profession were set apart from the rest of the population. We should not use profanity, get drunk, or take God's name in vain. I believed in the fallacy of perfection—we should be role models who could do no wrong.

Sitting in my first Braille class at the Center for the Visually Impaired with knots in my stomach, I felt like a kindergartner on her first day at school.

The Braille teacher introduced herself as Pam. As she handed me my Braille lesson book, she told me about her education and that she had been blind since birth. She introduced me to her guide dog, Rocky, who was sitting at her feet.

I was both fascinated by her ability to cope and scared of the road ahead of me. "Yes, ma'am," was all I could muster.

When I touched the Brailler, I noticed the six keys were wide (larger than my fingers) with a short space bar between them. It had a roller above the characters, much like the old-fashioned typewriter I used in typing class in 1958. I had seen one of these Brailler machines in a story about Helen Keller entitled *The Miracle Worker*. It certainly wasn't sleek and modern. Pam taught me to roll the stiff paper into the machine and slide the bar over to the left to begin typing.

As I was practicing my Braille, I thought about Louis Braille. *Here I am using this unique invention, and the man who created it never knew how many lives he would enrich.* I had read about the inventor of this system allowing blind people to read and write when I was a teacher, never imagining that one day I would be learning to use his method.

Louis Braille, who became blind at an early age, used the very tool that had caused his blindness to create his revolutionary alphabet in the nineteenth century when he was only a teenager. His was an inspiring story of creativity resulting from a disabling condition. Here's a synopsis: At the age of three, while playing in his father's workshop, he scratched one eye, which resulted in a blinding infection that spread to both eyes. While attending a school for blind youth, one of the first of its kind in the world, he heard a speaker describe an invention that allowed soldiers to share secret information on the battlefield without having to speak. It was a form of raised lettering made of dots and dashes, and it inspired the boy to think of a similar system that could work for blind people. Using the very awl from his father's occupation of crafting saddles and harnesses from leather, young Braille developed his six-dot system that allowed recognition of letters with a single fingertip. These six dots, raised as bumps, made it possible for blind people to read by touch. When Braille died of tuberculosis at the age of forty-three, no Paris newspaper wrote of his death. Six months later the institute, where he had been a teacher himself and was greatly admired by his pupils, finally adopted his six-dot method. Soon his system of raised dots became the world-wide standard.

I snapped back to hear Pam describe the six oval keys in front of me. These represent the cells or spaces arranged to form characters in Braille letters or characters of the alphabet. As I placed three fingers of both hands on the keys, I thought this was ingenuous. I couldn't imagine how I could master it.

My fingers strained to hit the keys correctly. To type "R," I pressed the middle key with my right hand while depressing all three with my left. It was just the opposite for "W." I marveled how "H" was the mirror image of "J." "F" mirrored "D," and "I" was the reflection of "E." When I tried to type "R," I got my left and right hands mixed up and typed "W" instead. By the end of the day I just wanted to go to sleep.

Slow and tedious but fascinating. I started getting the hang of it after a couple of weeks.

Reading was another story. I learned that I needed to use a light, steady movement of my two index fingers across the page. At first, reading a sentence would take me as long as ten minutes. The task of running my sore index fingers across the bumps on the stiff paper droned on. When Pam finished with her other student, I began the finger reading. *Let your fingers do the walking!* I repeated this mantra to myself over and over, never having been so bored in my life.

Once I timed myself. It had taken me thirty minutes to read five sentences. I began to think this marvelous invention was too old-fashioned for me. Would I ever master this archaic strategy for reading?

One day I heard a whoosh, whoosh sound. I asked Pam, "What are you doing?"

"I'm reading a magazine."

I quipped, "Wow! When I was a teacher, they wouldn't allow me to read for pleasure in the classroom."

She laughed and replied, "I was just trying to break the monotony."

Thinking of myself as a teacher seemed like another world.

Each day I went home and plopped on the bed with my Braille book. My assignment was to read for two hours. That would be four pages. I can't tell you how stressed and frustrated I felt. Some days I wanted to beat my head against the wall and scream, "I can't do this!"

Shame on you, Fiona. I realized if it hadn't been for all the people who helped me get into the CVI program—plus the Kiwanis Club members who were driving me—I wouldn't even have this opportunity. *Too many people to let down.*

One Monday morning as my Kiwanis volunteer helped me with my coat, he noticed my Braille book. Curious, he opened it and said, "Oh, I see it has the sentences on the left and the Braille on the right."

Lightbulb! That gave me an idea. All I had to do was memorize those printed words. The next day, I was ready. As my driver assisted me with my coat, I asked in my sweetest southern belle voice, "Could you read this page to me?"

He did. I clicked on the hidden tape recorder in my pocket. I could hardly wait to find my way to the school restroom. I sat on the john in the stall and listened to the recorded lesson. I was much better at memorizing than touching those blasted keys on a typewriter. Convincing myself this was an acceptable shortcut, I practiced my memory trick.

Each day that week, I tapped my way straight into the restroom as soon as I arrived in the building. I wasn't yet adept at walking with a cane, but now I was motivated by my secret task. With only five minutes until the bell, I hid in the stall and listened to my recorder until I had memorized the lesson for the day.

When I got to class, I put my two index fingers on the Braille, poised to read.

"Fiona, you're reading with such fluency," Pam commented.

Pleased, I zipped through the lesson.

After a few days, Pam caught on but she didn't tell me.

As soon as I arrived one morning, Pam's first words were, "The director wants to see you in his office."

"Right now?"

Her reply was terse. "Yes."

Pam gave me directions to the elevator and told me the number of steps to the "principal's office." All the way, I sensed that simply walking there was punishment for something. *Oh, no, Pam was onto my trick.*

Tapping my way to the elevator, I felt the beads of sweat popping out on my forehead. I pushed the button, listened for the door to open, and stepped inside. When I stepped off at the second floor I ran into someone who asked, "Can I help you?" I lost count and was in the wrong room. This kind person redirected me across the hall.

The director was expecting me. "Well, Fiona, what would you like to know?"

I didn't know what I would like to know when he asked that question. The first thing out of my mouth was "What color is your tie?" as if I knew he had on a tie.

He had no idea the color of his tie. He was blind like me. I knew his name was Scott and that he was a runner and a skier because my friend Elayne knew him, but this was not the time for chitchat.

Could I have been the first to ever cheat at Braille? I was embarrassed. Here I was—a teacher! A teacher doesn't cheat. Horrors! What would my students think?

Scott and I chatted for a while. Then the dreaded topic, "You do not have to take Braille if you don't want to. You can take something else, like cooking or macramé or guitar lessons."

I was grateful he didn't embarrass me by telling me he knew what I had done. I agreed that Braille wasn't for everyone. "It's archaic," I said, foolishly.

It became apparent that Braille was a necessity one day when my son pointed out the red circles around my eyes. I had picked up my red lip liner thinking I was using an eye liner. I had outlined my eyes in red and used the eyeliner on my lips. I needed to identify my makeup pencils. Shortly after that I was lamenting my frustration with the owner of a store that sold aids for the blind. He called me to the back of his shop to let me in on a little secret. "Have you ever heard of jumbo Braille?"

"Nope."

"I didn't think so. They don't tell anyone."

Like this was a big conspiracy, he demonstrated using a Perkins Brailler and label-making tape. This Braille was twice as large as Grade 1 Braille. I could feel the bumps!

We conspired. He sold me a jumbo brailler. Fancy that! He had just the thing for me.

CVI never knew. I can now make Braille labels for just about any object. I Braille my makeup pencils and canned goods. I label food, spices, prescriptions, and office folders. You may be wondering why I would Braille file folders. I feel a sense of power when I can find my own printed matter even if I can't read it.

I created my own system of Braille by using fabric glue or puff paint to identify the colors of my clothing. For example, the letter "A," one bump, is for black, the letter "B," two vertical bumps, is for blue. I've found that creating systems for remembering things is what works for me. Different shapes, textures, and sizes represent things. Instead of having all Braille dots on my computer I have a large Velcro square for "Enter" and a large round bump for "Insert."

I failed to learn to read a book in Braille. However, today I certainly respect—and use—Louis Braille's ingenious system in my own way.

11

Freedom of Choice

Do you remember the "Footprints" poem? It was the inspiration for my sixth chapter title. I've always enjoyed another ditty that goes like this: "I had the blues, because I had no shoes, until upon the street, I met a man who had no feet." Like "Footprints," the authorship of this one can't be proven.

I believe in the importance of finding new ways to feel free and have choices. Disability is tough to manage. We can "feel disabled" just by getting older and unable to live on our own. We feel disabled when we make bad choices and find ourselves incarcerated. Never mind that we may have done this to ourselves. We still feel helpless and inadequate. Our limitations can become chains.

I have been asked, "What do you miss the most since you lost your eyesight?"

I miss the freedom to make choices I could make when I could see.

Freedom is so important. When I was first blind, I often was frustrated because I had so few choices. I had lost the choice to do what I wanted . . . when I wanted.

My friends and family would say, "Fiona, you are too demanding!"

My counselor would say, "No, you are communicating to others what you need—it's a fact of life that you are dependent in some ways. You will need to learn how to let others know what you need."

I read a book by an author who was blind. I agree with a lot of what she said. For example, I wish other people would understand that being disabled does not mean we want to be dependent on people all the time. What this author wished for was the freedom of choice—to be able to say: "Today I feel like doing it myself." Her analogy was running an errand . . . maybe today, maybe tomorrow. In other words, she would do it herself, on her own terms, rather than relying on the schedule of a helper, no matter how well meaning that helper might be.

One doesn't have to be blind, crippled, or mentally challenged to want the freedom to make choices. This applies to the spiritually or emotionally wounded, too.

Someone who has lost a child, a job, a limb, or the ability to function easily among people needs to be able to say, "I need time out," or "How about a hug?" I have friends who have lost loved ones or suffered mental collapse. Some even suffer in silence, unable to communicate their pain.

Today I feel strong; tomorrow I may not. Please give me the freedom to be independent today or needy tomorrow. Freedom of choice. That's what it's all about.

I have a hard time explaining to my friends and family that some days I feel strong enough to walk across the room to get something I need, and other days I wish someone would do it for me. Some days I can use my cane and walk alone. Other days I appreciate hanging onto an arm.

Don't all people, disabled or not, have days like this? What are friends for?

I remember another saying with an anonymous origin: "Pain is inevitable. Suffering is optional." I heard it quoted by a presidential candidate of the '50s, Adlai Stevenson.

• • •

My mother is a prime example of one who showed faith and courage in the face of adversity. She was told that she was the first female to walk on two prosthetic legs. I cannot imagine being fourteen with two wooden legs. What's even more amazing is that she is the one who—as a teenager—made the choice to have her deformed legs amputated.

In 1925, a person with a disability didn't even go to school, much less graduate with a scholarship for college. Mama hitchhiked to a nearby business school where she studied to become a legal secretary and bookkeeper. She excelled and was asked to teach the courses of her trade. She walked without crutches and often fell on rough pavement.

When she was a child she crawled or pushed herself along on the low-to-the-ground platform her father built for her as a mode of transportation while she was at school. It broke my heart when she described this to me, and I wondered if her classmates ever made fun of her.

Mama made friends easily. She and her friends played tag by her jumping on one of the backs of the girls so she could feel like she was running, too. She told me all this without bitterness. I never heard Mama gripe or complain.

My sister and I never thought of Mama as handicapped. She did everything other mothers did. In some ways, she did more. She sewed all our clothes, cooked delicious meals, and mopped her floors. She worked as a bookkeeper. In later years, she ran three businesses at once—our family restaurant, a sitter service for the sick, and a tax preparation business. She never let on if she felt rejection, disappointment, fear, or even the least bit weird about how funny she walked. She just smiled and did it. "I trust God with my fate" was her mantra. The best part was she knew how to laugh!

My mother never made me feel like she didn't have choices. In my eyes, she was capable of anything.

I thought I had a good hold on my situation at Easter when I turned to my mother at dinner with all the family and announced, "I have been blind for six months. I have had a few lessons in mobility. I know I can handle being handicapped, Mama!"

My mother sat there for a moment. She said, "Fiona, I am not handicapped. You can't miss something you never had. You have lost your eyesight. That is truly a loss and a handicap." I'll never forget that. Mama, my blessing, you are in my heart every day.

When she was eighty-five years old we were featured together in the book, *Portraits in Spirit: Honoring 25 Disabled Georgians.* Mama was living in Garden View, an assisted living home owned by my sister, when the book was on exhibit at the 1996 Paralympics Games.

Determined to attend the opening of the exhibit, Mama didn't wait for anyone else to make arrangements for her to attend. She called the airline and told them about the festivities and how she was to be honored. My mother had never called for a flight reservation much less flown in an airplane, but she was determined. She was so excited that she picked up the phone and somehow figured out who to contact.

If my mother wanted to do something, there was no stopping her. She didn't make a big deal about it—she just did it. AirTran gave her a free ticket and rolled out the red carpet. When we arrived at the airport, she showed the airport personnel how to put the heavy batteries back onto her electric wheelchair which she had been using since Daddy died five years earlier.

This amazing woman thrilled my heart when she came to Mississippi for the Ms. American Classic Woman pageant in 2005. She was not disappointed that I was first runner-up. That night I danced with my mother, leaning on her as she maneuvered her electric wheelchair. I will never forget that evening.

Mama was part of every day of my life in my mind and my soul . . . my hero through childhood moments, accomplishments, disappointments, college, my traumatic surgery, and my challenging years of blindness. Before her death she saw the growth that brought me full face into the person I am: creative, loving, demanding (at times), very thankful, plus determined to be productive and to love people just as they are. She was my anchor for positive thinking . . . my tower of strength.

Mama died on March 1, 2006—she was ninety-four years old.

12

Autograph Your Life with Purpose

I can relate to Mark Twain's comment that "You can't depend on your eyes when your imagination is out of focus."

Creativity has its downside. I have so much enthusiasm that I tend to spirit many ideas, more than I am able to juggle. Suddenly feeling tired and overwhelmed, I realize I have too many items on my plate. Staying focused is my challenge. Being purposeful is my goal.

As a storyteller, I sometimes provide what's called the back story. In this chapter I'm going to flash forward a bit.

Three years after the events on that tragic night which resulted in my going blind, I sat in a courtroom. The hours and days wore on with three weeks of grueling, boring, dry testimony. It was my life, my tragedy, and even I was bored. How could any layperson sitting on a jury of my peers understand all the medical gibberish?

The lawsuit was torture for me at every level. Friends and family members attending the trial would report how they thought that day's testimony went. My skin crawled as a friend described two young women who chatted and filed their nails, oblivious to their duties as jurors. I was shocked they got away with it. I expected more from our judicial system.

I also expected a just outcome and, frankly, a sum of money that would compensate me for medical mistakes that cost me my eyesight, my career, my income, my retirement . . . and to some extent my identity as a productive citizen.

I will not provide specific names and dollar figures, but I want my readers to know that I fought for the justice every American would expect in a situation like mine. Yet I did not receive it. I did receive a settlement from the manufacturer of the instrument.

People told me the doctors should have been ashamed of how they protected themselves, instead of me, their patient, for whom they had taken the Hippocratic Oath to practice medicine ethically, to place my health above all else. Others said even the hospital had let me down because they did not have emergency plans in place. I just nodded and listened, as my well-meaning friends spoke.

In my heart, I knew all that and more. I knew that life is not always fair. I knew I had to be my own advocate. And, in time, I knew I had to get on with my life.

Years later I see the purpose for this time in my life even clearer. My dear family doctor, the one I call Dr. Right, said this: "Fiona, most people would rather be dead than blind. God has a plan for you. You could not have achieved it sighted or you would still be sighted."

As I listened, I agreed. Generally, the things that do us the most good, we see as bad. When we have good things happen to us, we become careless, assuming life will always be good like it is now. That weakens our resolve to be on guard, to remain spiritually strong and devoted to the truth of our faith. Unless we are faced with adversity, we often don't develop good character. In Romans 5:3-4 we read that

" . . . *we also rejoice in our sufferings, because we know that suffering produces perseverance; perseverance, character; and character, hope.*"

Dr. Right was kind to add this encouragement: "A large percentage of our society says, 'If not for you, I would be okay.' You did not say that, Fiona. You got on with your life."

One more comment I want my readers to consider. I believe the trial I endured had an unjust outcome. But, if you find yourself feeling pity for me, please stop that thought immediately and consider the trials of our Lord which led to the innocent Lamb of God being slain on the cross.

No comparison.

Once the lawsuit was behind me, the dreams of what I would do when I finally had all the money I needed faded away. I didn't have all the money I needed. But I had all that God thought I needed. Of course, it would take years for me to have this level of wisdom and insight.

Immediately after the trial, I was stunned. Where would I go from here? I had no financial sense. Advice came from all sides on how to invest the settlement so I could have a decent income the rest of my life.

After the disappointing outcome of the case, my attorney arranged a week's vacation on his yacht in the Bahamas for Jerry and me plus my best friends, Pat and Marie. While everyone else was deep sea fishing, I sat on the boat pondering what to do next. Maybe get married since the lawsuit was over? My life had been on hold for three years waiting for the legal issues to be resolved. Jerry and I had been dating for five years, and now we could move forward. I'd always clung to the idea he and I would get married, but now I wondered if he really wanted to live with a woman who was so needy. Someone had to drive me wherever I wanted to go—and I wanted to go places all the time. I fiercely wanted to live as normally as possible.

So many questions! Jerry was overwhelmed, working full-time and keeping up with my needs.

Plus, after three years of waiting for the ordeal of the lawsuit to end and now the shock of losing it, I focused on the house I dreamed of having. Two things had held me together—planning a romantic fairy tale wedding and having a castle in which to share our love.

I invested in a house, quietly hoping Jerry would want to be there instead of having me move in to his house. It was spacious with four bedrooms, high ceilings, and lots of windows. I liked the open living area even though it was difficult for me to navigate without the typical box-shaped rooms to trail the walls with my knuckles. I bought new living room furniture to bang my shins on. The sunlight shining through the house gave me a sense of being outside.

Jerry, the ultra-conservative, thought it would be wiser to move in with him and invest in stocks and bonds. He probably would have married me sooner if I had listened to him.

It wasn't a practical move. My house was too big, and it cost more money to furnish than I imagined. I wanted to decorate and play—I hadn't played in so long. I wanted to spend time shopping and laughing with my girlfriends, to entertain my family comfortably, and to create a business. I needed to be professionally productive. And I needed the income.

Young Audiences of Atlanta was booking me into schools and I had plenty of work. The fellowship had kept me in storytelling gigs during the three-year discovery period of the lawsuit.

Now I needed direction. I had no idea of how to build a business and no idea that being blind made it doubly hard to manage. I was facing monumental tasks and didn't even understand that. I served on the Board of the Center for the Visually Impaired, and I was President of Southern Order of Storytellers. I took computer classes, learned to use Quicken accounting software, and took a comedy class. Somehow I found time for Jerry. Could there be any doubt why I was tired all the time?

I was asked to be on the Tommy Nobis Center board and SOS wanted me back on their board, but keeping up with information was nearly impossible for me. I couldn't do the simple things that sighted people take for granted such as writing down a phone number, being able to find where you put it, and then reading it again. Prescriptions, documents, checks, and information including current events were just not easily accessible to me.

It seemed logical to hire someone to help me. I didn't know if I could afford a twenty-four hour per week personal assistant, but I wanted one. I didn't have a marketing or business plan—I just did it.

Kathy Davis appeared in my life somehow through friends in Duluth where I had last taught. Kathy and I agreed to try to start a speaking business for six months. She would have many tasks as my assistant to handle every part of my waking day—accounting, wardrobe, nails, hair, and managing a household even though I was the only one in it. I hoped Kathy would find more opportunities for me to speak. Kathy was a young woman right out of college with a marketing degree and a lot of initiative. She had a baby girl, so it was an ideal job for her.

It was up to me to give my assistant direction, and I didn't know where to begin. How do you develop contacts? I got ideas, pitched them to Kathy, and waited for her to take the ball and run with it. It didn't work. We were distracted by storytelling gigs which continued to come my way and my up and down moods.

Focusing was difficult, because I was fighting depression. Some days Kathy came to work to find me still in bed. I never admitted how depressed I was. My life had been a whirlwind since I first became blind. That made it easy to avoid grieving for my loss of sight. I was spent with just getting through each day as I adapted. Often I imagined how much longer it took me than a sighted person to do everyday things. I finally realized if I dwelled on that I would never get out of bed.

In front of an audience I didn't "feel" disabled nor did I look it, I was told. On the stage, in the classroom, and behind a podium, I felt normal, happy, and not blind. When I wasn't there, I was tired and lost.

Looking back, I see this as my denial period. I was not accepting blindness as my challenge but instead as an inconvenience that I lived with.

So many times I was given responsibility for something I had no idea how I could accomplish. Yet I couldn't bring myself to tell them I was afraid I couldn't do it, so I accepted.

In 1992 Carmen Deedy asked me to co-produce the Atlanta Storytelling Festival at the Atlanta History Center. I had produced the Olde Christmas Festival in January of 1990 and asked Carmen to co-produce. Now it was her turn to call on me for help.

Carmen suggested I be one of the storytellers. When the day of the festival arrived, I was sitting in one of the outdoor tents waiting to tell a story. I heard my colleague, B.J. Abraham, introducing me. Suddenly I felt sick. I wanted to run. I couldn't run without holding on to Jean, my sighted guide. I turned to her and said, "Get me out of here, quick." She didn't know what was up, but she gave me her arm and we headed for the main building at a fast pace. I thought I would pass out before I got away from the crowd. I didn't know what was happening. When we entered the building, my legs floated out from under me. I collapsed.

When I came to, my heart was thumping wildly. As my chest tightened I felt like I was going to explode. Two volunteers who had medical experience rushed to my side and laid me on the floor of the great hall. I recognized one of them as my friend Joan. As she leaned into me I grabbed her arm, "I'm having a heart attack," I stammered.

Joan said, "No, you're having an anxiety attack, Fiona." Although she was an RN, I still didn't believe her. Even as I write this, my chest tightens as I recall how I felt that night. Remember how my superior vena cava had been patched with a piece of my heart lining? I was convinced the day would come when it would break open.

"My heart's going to burst."

Joan tried to comfort me. "The EMTs are on their way. You're going to be fine."

The ambulance screamed as it swung in. They lifted me and whizzed off.

Warm pee wet my legs and dripped down my thighs. Crying, I spoke to the EMT, "I'm dying." Somehow I recalled reading that losing control of your bladder meant death.

"No," she replied, but I don't know what else she said. All I could think was I would never see my family again.

My family doctor was waiting for me at the hospital. He assured me I was not dying. I was only scared, but to this day I don't know why. Was it a delayed reaction to the previous four years and the grueling trial?

Ever since that fateful night in the ER, I had been running, running, trying to be "super blind." I wanted to be as brave as my mother. I did everything the way I thought my mother would. She had been a businesswoman all her adult life. She worked with numbers (accounting) and loved it. I couldn't even balance my checkbook after becoming blind. I needed help.

Time to slow down. I needed proficiency in computer skills, mobility, and taking care of my needs like cooking and paying bills. I now understand my erratic behavior was because I had no direction.

The next year Kathy left my employment for a teaching position. Having been inside so many schools with me, she decided that would be a great career for her. I was happy for her, but now I had no driver or daily assistant.

God always sent me angels when I needed them. My storytelling buddies, Ann and B.J., started a consortium. We called it Atlanta Storyworks. Together we did performances and presentations on storytelling skills. We traveled as the act, "Three Stories High," and told Aesop fables and international tales.

Over the next two years, B.J. and I performed in tandem for the National Storytelling Conference. The sad part of this story was, as artists, we were unable to discipline ourselves to be marketers. This is a thorn for many creative people. Eventually, we disbanded and pursued different paths. Alas, Atlanta Storyworks was no more, but I gained confidence as an entrepreneur and performing artist.

The summer following the demise of Atlanta Storyworks I sat at my computer, pondering what my purpose truly was to be. There were so many storytellers—I needed a niche. I remembered the summer I spent with a young protégé researching stories that exemplified good character. *That's it! We need tales about good character.*

When I had lived in Oregon in the '70s I wasn't teaching but instead spent my time exploring creative avenues. I discovered a series of tapes by Marlo Thomas about liking yourself. At the time her show, *That Girl*, was among the most popular shows on TV. She and her father, Danny Thomas, were well respected as role models for our generation. She inspired my creativity. Thus, the program "Be Who You Are" was born to encourage kids to be the best they could be.

Heather Forest greatly influenced my story work. She was an internationally known performing artist. Early in my career, after I became blind, she encouraged me by recommending me for performances in the Chicago area. Through her referrals I toured the northern and central regions of Illinois.

With Heather Forest's permission, I took a story that she had brought to life from her interpretation of an Aesop fable. My version of "Charlie Macaroni" was birthed. The crow in the story thinks he is ugly. As the story grew with my experience of telling it to hundreds of children, I was inspired to use it as the pivot point for "Be Who You Are." Eventually the story emerged with its own personality.

When I had taught elementary school, I often sang songs about being confident and liking yourself. A journey of healing was emerging. I was the one who longed to fit in, to feel pretty, not ugly.

In "Charlie Macaroni," the crow sees his image in the pond.

Now I longed to see my image.

Flashing forward to explain more about how my storytelling career continued to flourish . . .

By the early and mid-1990s Atlanta was all abuzz about hosting the Olympic Games in 1996. This would include a series of athletic contests for people with disabilities, known as the Atlanta Paralympics. With these approaching, the director and founder of Young Audiences wrote a lovely bio to introduce me as one of their storytellers. In the fall of 1995 the Paralympics Executive Committee invited me to tell the story of their mascot, Blaze. He was eight feet tall and fun to dance with in front of the kids. I traveled to schools in metro Atlanta with many Paralympics athletes. Speaking on the same platform with world-class athletes was an honor and a privilege. In 1996 I was invited to perform at the Atlanta Paralympics Games. I entertained at the evening event for the athletes and their families from around the world.

Each storytelling gig told me I enjoyed speaking with the stories to back up my presentation. I pioneered the first example of presenting character traits in a creative form for Georgia students. My program about self-worth and discovering our gifts and talents was popular with students of all ages. I was asked to add an extra presentation for a special class. We talked about what it is like to be different. I pulled out of my repertoire a funny old southern folktale with my own twist. My signature story, "Billy Bowlegs," had special meaning for students with challenges. Billy Bowlegs was a wiener dog who soared even though he was disabled and couldn't run in the same way other dogs ran. The obstacle was that he couldn't do what he loved—chase rabbits. But Billy discovered a way—meeting his challenge and overcoming it.

The children loved it so much that I realized why I wanted to tell it. The story spoke to my own struggles and to my mother's inability to run and play like normal children. Billy Bowlegs had a new purpose.

One particular third grader who happened to be named Billy caught the tennis ball that I threw into the audience. The teachers collectively held their breath. Billy, a visually impaired student, had a tendency to act out inappropriately. Remarkably, Billy and I connected on a different level. What beautiful communication! Together we demonstrated the use of Braille and sighted guide technique. I know that neither Billy nor I will forget that moment.

Another teacher came by the second day I was telling stories at her school. She had a small group of children with special needs at the program the day before. The teacher shared, "I asked the class what they remembered most about your performance. The boy with Asperger's syndrome [the high end of the spectrum for autism] said 'It's okay to be different.'" Words I will not soon forget.

The title, "Autograph Your Life with Purpose," emerged when an assistant named Cookie and I were laughing and cooling our heels in the mall. We checked out our usual places—coffee shop and dollar store. I was trying to come up with a title for my business cards.

Cookie said, "Okay, let's browse the card shop for ideas. She saw a greeting card that inspired me to create the branding for my business, "Autograph Your Life with Purpose." Purpose and people have been my focus. I love people, and I live for a purpose!

Cookie and I worked together for several years. I still smile when I hear her quip with twisted words like "mental pause." She could take a simple yo-yo and mesmerize the kids with her antics. But she did not want the spotlight. Warming up the audience was all she wanted to do as I got ready for them. Her prayers and her personality gave me energy. The storytelling and school markets continued to draw me in, but I still wanted to speak to adults.

Word of mouth spread—my phone rang for speeches. People wanted to hear what happened to me. I had to have some training to get beyond the emotional ownership of the story. Joining the Georgia Chapter of the National Speakers Association (NSA) would be my new adventure. With sweaty palms, just like when I used to hold hands with a boy in the Royal Theater, I nervously stood up at my first meeting to introduce myself. I wanted to be just like these professionals but how would I meet them? In a large group like this, greeting people was really tenuous. I could not discern who was talking to whom and when to jump in on a conversation.

My colleague, Ann, from Atlanta Storyworks, took me to the first few NSA Georgia meetings. Ann was good at taking notes and networking with people. I attended a seminar about the business of speaking and was blown away by Gail Geary, a former attorney and teacher. I once had the erroneous notion that teachers could do nothing but teach. But Gail inspired me to acknowledge my potential. I attended as many seminars as I could.

Then I found a friend in NSA. Rene Godfrey made me feel accepted in the organization. He was new himself, yet had an uncanny ability to connect with people. When I heard Rene's story of wretched poverty in Haiti and how he reached his desire for U.S. citizenship, I was overwhelmed. If he could conquer those odds, I could hurdle mine!

Encouraged to join in and share my own talents, I volunteered to instruct at the Speakers Academy about using stories in public speaking. I had a business card designed with my new logo, "Autograph Your Life with Purpose." My own autograph was above it. My mission was, and is, to share my personal story to encourage others to accept difficult changes in their lives. Once again I was spurred on.

Ironically, my teenage neighbor, Andrew, while browsing my Senior Class yearbook, asked, "Did you always want to be a speaker?"

I said, "No."

"It says here that you want to be a public speaker."

"Really?" I was surprised because I didn't remember that. Must have been a whim!

Recently, B.J. and I were reminiscing about all the events that have taken place since my blindness. She exclaimed, "Fiona, you amaze me! You are a realist and a dreamer!"

"How do you mean? I see that as such a contradiction."

She protested, "No, it's a compliment. It's a balance."

Me balanced? Maybe she was right. It surprised me when my friends told me the affect I had on people. Having a mother with a physical disability who saw herself as normal made me think the same way. God let me live for His greater purpose. I like to think we grow and learn from our mistakes. Being aware of my limitations is still an uphill battle for me. What others view as impossible feats, I see as another hurdle to jump. I thank my mother for that insight. She has been the constant inspiration which spurs me on.

13

Laugh to Keep from Crying

This chapter will make you laugh, and it will make you cry. Life is like that, isn't it? It hands us some crazy circumstances. And you'll find that disabled people are not immune from comic moments . . . as well as life's troubles.

So here's a series of vignettes to provide insight into my life as a blind person. It can be hilarious at times, especially if you surround yourself with people who have a healthy sense of humor, which I try to do. Some of my stories elicit such mirth that people have even given them their own names, such as the pocketbook story you're about to read.

The crying part? I'll save that for the end.

My friend Teresa took me to Lenox Square Mall to shop. I complained as we linked arms and strolled by her favorite store. "I can't go shopping. I can't *see!*"

"Hush, girlfriend, I know you can do it!"

We entered Pendleton's—a store I had passed by before but never entered, because I'm not the preppy type.

Teresa put my hands on a rack of skirts, shirts, and slacks. I thought Pendleton's was a sweater store. As I stood there, I thought I should act like I'm looking. I fingered each garment. *Okay, Fiona, pretend you see something you like.* My imagination went to work. As I touched the fabrics, I guessed what color they might be. I checked out the stitching and quality of the workmanship. I was new to being blind and still learning what touch could reveal. *Hey, I might catch on to this kind of shopping! I can go by texture.*

I was so engrossed I forgot about my friend. Excitement tingled in my heart. I turned to the right and reached into the darkness for a new rack to feel. *Hmmm, I didn't know Pendleton's sold purses.* I ran my fingers down the smooth leather strap to the shoulder bag's zipper. I unzipped the purse, stuck my hand inside and . . . removed a set of car keys!

Teresa shouted from across the store, "Fiona, that's not me!"

Frozen, I tried to recover with a joke. "Now I've got a car and don't know where it's parked!" I was hoping the person who belonged to the purse would speak. She didn't. I dropped the keys, forced a smile, and cried to Teresa, "Get me outta here!"

She and I linked arms and ran out of the store. Teresa told me the lady with the unzipped purse just stared at me, licking her ice cream cone. All I knew was that she never made a sound.

"You should have seen her face!"

"Didn't she know I couldn't see?"

"No, Fiona. She didn't know you're *blind!* She probably thought you were trying to steal from her. You don't *look* blind at all."

"I don't?"

"No, but you sure looked like a pickpocket!"

That was my first lesson about accepting who I had become. I needed to be assertive about my disability—taking charge of my life and getting over feeling pitiful in public. It was up to me to make others feel comfortable with me, not the other way around.

• • •

The early days of getting back into storytelling were intense. Nights of restless sleep, tight shoulders, and worry, wondering if I could "pull off" a performance without sight. You may remember Carmen from the last chapter. I first met her when she joined the Southern Order of Storytellers. I was the President of SOS at the time. She called me out of the blue and asked for advice.

Carmen was a natural and destined for great things. I was amazed at her gift for words. We hung out together, and she took me to perform at a Mensa meeting. I asked her to co-direct the Southern Order of Storytelling festival in January. She asked me to help with an idea she had for a play featuring the two of us.

Carmen and I spent many hours planning "Southern Comfort." Carmen wrote it, and I collaborated. We performed the two-woman show for bookstores and colleges. But getting ready was a challenge. Sometimes I had trouble arranging transportation or learning my lines, because I was so dependent on others. I was inexperienced with the computer. The only way to keep up with memorizing my part was to use a tape recorder, but I hated rewinding to hunt for a certain line. Everything was tedious. I wouldn't admit my problems nor would I ask for help. However, the project gave me a new purpose after the fellowship had ended. Plus, I'd been blind over a year and still tired easily. But hanging out with Carmen rejuvenated me.

One night I met Carmen in Macon for our first major show. The play was about two elderly sisters. Carmen was the comic, and I was the straight woman. We made my character a little near-sighted to cover my blindness. At this point, I wasn't ready to draw attention to my disability. I refused to use my cane.

That night at Macon College I sat backstage trying to think of a clever entrance for Carmen and me. She peeked out and said, "It's a full house—seven hundred!"

We planned to step out from behind the velvet curtain and introduce our characters, then walk onto the set as the curtain opened.

"How are you going to get backstage again? Take my arm?" Carmen asked.

"No, I'd look helpless. We have to fake this. I know—I'll stand close to your right shoulder, barely touching. On cue, we'll both turn inward and I'll follow your lead through the center of the closed curtains." I showed her how we would do this. We practiced over and over, getting tickled each time.

Curtains up! "Welcome, everyone..." we bantered. I felt a tension in the auditorium, but didn't know the reason was because I was inching closer to the edge of the orchestra pit in front of us. It was a long way down, but I didn't even know it was there. Carmen was fidgeting, I didn't understand why. We closed our intro, and I spun toward Carmen. I was a second ahead of cue. While Carmen was still facing forward, I grabbed her right breast! Shocked, I blurted out, "Doorknob!"

It brought down the house. Seven hundred people laughed and relaxed. They became an audience who was with us, not just watching . . . anticipating disaster. The night was splendid. The show was the epitome of perfection. I don't think we could have made it happen quite like that again.

One August after Jerry and I were married, we went whitewater rafting on the Nantahala River with his office buddies, my sister's husband, and some other friends. It took a lot of talking on Jerry's part to convince me to go. I kept asking, "Are you certain I'll be safe?"

"Sure," he said. "I called their reservation office and asked. Relax."

I didn't know too many in his group and was nervous about this adventure. Obviously, I trusted Jerry, because he always watched out for my safety, but I was neither athletic nor a good swimmer. He also worked to help me stretch my limits. As we waited in line for our raft, Jerry whispered, "Hide your cane."

"What? I thought you checked to be sure it's okay for a blind person to do this."

"Oh. Sure." And then he laughed.

This was Jerry's way of trying to make me feel normal—kidding me. However, I was praying I would make it through this adventure. Imagine lunging down a choppy river in a raft with your eyes closed! Who does that?

With help, I scrambled aboard the six-man raft behind another couple and sat down beside Jerry. I was eager to ask the others: "Are you sure this is safe?" The guide assured me he would be right behind me and would jump in to save me if needed. As we shoved off, I maintained a death grip on the edge of the raft. My feet were crammed so far under the sides, I'm sure I could have flipped us over if I started to tumble.

My brother-in-law thought he would break the ice with a cool trick. He grabbed hold of the first branch we floated under. To his surprise we were not merely floating, we were racing like maniacs down the river. Not realizing how fast the rapids were moving us, he was left suspended in midair. His back-up plan was to drop into the next raft with some friends. No such luck! They were long gone too. We giggled at the spectacle of Harvey dangling. He had to drop into a group of strangers—Japanese tourists. Then he waited for an opportunity to jump in the water and catch up with his raft. Bet he won't do that again!

The trip down was thrilling. My heart leaped with the raft on the final turn before our lunch break. We had made it halfway. The ladies got out and stood around talking while the guys banked the rafts, then they rejoined us.

People were standing near me, but I wasn't sure who. For reassurance, I reached for the edge of Jerry's swim trunks—anything to hold on to. The gal next to me started a conversation. Others standing around joined in. As often happens, someone asked the question,

"How did you become blind?" Well, I love an audience, so I jumped into the story. Then I lightened the mood by telling them about the time I stuck my hand into that lady's purse at Pendleton's. I was on a roll. They were laughing and having fun. I liked the attention, but I also felt self-conscious. I twisted my finger around the hem of his swim trunks as I babbled on, twisting and turning like a coquettish teenager. I continued talking, never missing a beat.

Finally, someone who knew me leaned in my direction. "Fiona, that's not Jerry beside you."

I let go and babbled, "I'm so sorry." Too late. The young man walked off, perplexed, I'm sure.

They teased me all afternoon about feeling strange men.

Finally, one of the gals confided, "Fiona, I don't think that guy knows you're blind."

I just smiled.

On most occasions when we were together, Jerry insisted I carry my cane although I didn't really need it with him along as my sighted guide. His reasoning was sound. Even with me on his arm, people couldn't tell I was blind, and they weren't always paying attention, especially in crowded places such as malls. Sometimes they would plow right into me, but the cane would serve as a warning . . . in most cases.

I'm grateful that Jerry paid close attention to my safety. He also made me comfortable by teasing me. His sense of humor, especially in those first years after I lost my sight, helped me when I was nervous or scared.

One year we went to Fort Lauderdale with a couple named Paul and Teresa who loved the beach. Paul asked if I would go up in a parasail if he paid for it. I had never seen parasailing. He assured me of how safe it was. I doubt he knew that—he probably just thought it would be fun to watch me.

The talk went on all day until it was time for me to parasail. "Come on, Fiona. Teresa will be on the tube, riding out to the boat with you."

"What do you mean?" I thought everyone was going up.

Paul dodged my question by focusing on how I would be delivered safely to the boat. "They can't get any closer to shore with such a large boat. That's why they have such a big inner tube to deliver you. Come on—it's practically the size of a truck tire."

Teresa was very quiet. I could tell Jerry was pacing the beach. I later learned that he didn't like the idea but said nothing. Paul continued to taunt me, daring me to do it. Jerry was thinking I would figure out that Paul was ribbing me more than anything.

I didn't pick up on that, so I climbed onto the huge inner tube which zoomed toward the boat.

"Hey, where will you guys be?" I hollered.

"Oh, Jerry and I decided we'd rather ride on the jet skis."

The sensation of the tube roaring across the surf and my boarding the boat were enough to make me shout, "Stop! Take me back!"

But the assistant was kind and carefully strapped me into my harness. That's when I realized that Teresa wasn't with me, probably too scared to even ride from the shore to the boat. Parasailing meant I would be a hundred yards in the air alone and with no control over the parachute. I was on my own now, and it was decision time.

"What if the line snaps?"

"That's never happened," replied the assistant.

I took a deep breath and thought, *If God has kept me alive through all the trauma I've experienced, surely I'll make it back to the ground in one piece.*

I did it! I went parasailing, and I admit it was an incredible ride.

But the truth is I was praying the whole time.

• • •

Now for the crying. I promised honesty, so I'm jumping into the deep end . . .

More than twelve years had passed since Jerry and I met on that dance floor when I was newly divorced and trying to find my way. In that time, we had fallen in love, I had won the Christa McAuliffe Fellowship, I had become blind, I had endured a three-year lawsuit with a bad result, my dear father had died, my storytelling career had flourished, and Jerry and I had married. I'm sorry to say that by 1998, Jerry and I were divorced.

We are classic examples of why so many marriages don't work. Our initial attraction to each other was pure chemistry. The relationship strengthened in many ways during my surgery, its aftermath of blindness, and the court case. Jerry was completely supportive, always by my side. And when he was not, I longed for him. I recall thinking, *I need my love with me*, when the lawyers would not permit him in the courtroom. He was such a tower of strength, and—despite my feistiness—I needed him. In fact, I am sure I'm a challenge—needy in some ways because of my disability yet longing to be independent. And, as I have admitted, learning to submit—to God and, in a healthy way, to a spouse—has been a struggle. Yet I know it's the foundation for trust. Learning submission is like exercising a muscle—the more you work at it, the stronger you get. In 1998, I was not strong enough.

I can't speak for Jerry, but for me there was no rock bottom or eureka moment. It was a slow erosion of the commitment to make the marriage work. I am disappointed in myself—and Jerry, too—that we didn't learn to live alongside one another.

In my case, I can think of several reasons. I ask myself if these are excuses or influences worth exploring. I'll unpack a few, in case doing so will help readers who can relate.

Like everyone, I am the product of my growing-up years and my coming-of-age period when people choose mates. For me, the latter happened twice. In an upcoming chapter, I will share an example of the mixed messages many Southern men and women were sending each other in the years I was single between each of my two marriages. I must admit that I contributed to those mixed messages. I also didn't exercise the maturity to avoid situations which aren't productive for a single person longing for a suitable mate in a God-centered marriage. I had that goal, but I wasn't sure how to achieve it.

My expectations for marriage may have been unrealistic because of what I saw between my parents. My mother was strong, overpowering and yet full of grace. By comparison, my father seemed weak. Then I struggled through the young adult years of rebellion, thinking my mother was too demanding and misunderstanding how my father dealt with her. Looking back with more maturity, I realize what I perceived as my father's weakness was quiet strength. He was able to exercise restraint even when my mother did not. Of course, I had no first-hand knowledge of the give and take required in marriage, and I probably misinterpreted their interactions. I probably even judged them unfairly.

I carried these notions into my marriage to Jerry, having little understanding of how to be a mate. For his part, he, too, has flaws— who doesn't? Also, we could not find common ground in certain areas. I was grateful that Jerry is a Christian, but I wanted him to be with me at church. And as a creative woman, it was hard for me to accept some of my engineer husband's in-the-box thinking.

For too many years, my grounding in faith was shallow . . . I consider myself still craving the right path even as I write this. As the saying goes, God is not finished with me yet. I learn every day.

The story of Jerry and Fiona did not end in 1998 however. Another surprise is in store.

14

Close Encounters

In the '50s in the South, strangers were just viewed as nice people we didn't know yet. Today it's not that simple. How sad for us that we have to be so cautious about whom we meet and how we meet them. It's more difficult today to know how and when to respond or react. Now that I'm blind, I have an added dimension. I don't have the benefit of body language to make wise judgments about the people I encounter.

These are two stories of experiences from before and after my surgical incident. The first happened when I was forty years old and newly divorced and the other happened during my early recovery from blindness.

During a mid-life moment of eager singleness, I made a wrong choice. It seemed like it would be fun at the time. I shudder to think how it might have ended. This was the '80s when church socials for singles were virtually nonexistent. Dance clubs were the way for singles to meet singles. Since dancing was my hobby, I thought that was a good place to start my single-again life.

After the crushing blow of ending a nineteen-year marriage and seeing my husband with a younger woman, I needed to feel young again myself. How many of us go "out there" to seek validation, often without thought of the consequences?

His sandy hair fell over his boyish face in a charming way. One could say everything was charming about Boy Toy. He was a good dancer and could carry a conversation. He showered me with attention, which made it easy for me to give him my phone number.

High school *déjà vu* set in when he picked me up for our date. The black Pontiac Trans Am could have been a dead giveaway. Young? He still had peach fuzz on his face. Apologizing for the loud muffler, he explained that his car was in the shop. Reading my mind, he added, "My sixteen-year-old brother loaned me his."

Proud of his plans, Boy Toy informed me that we had reservations at the Polaris, a restaurant atop one of Georgia's finest hotels. *That will set him back a week's wages!* After dinner we would dance the night away on the revolving dance floor. How romantic! I felt like Cinderella, and years were melting off my psyche.

We got settled at the restaurant, and I ordered a glass of wine. Boy Toy jumped in with, "I'm in training, just a Coke for me."

"What kind of training?"

"Football."

I mused that it may be more like potty training. I was getting vibes that I was out with a baby rather than a babe. I rationalized that Boy Toy was one of those people who looks eternally young. I hoped he was at least thirty, since I was newly forty. Later I would learn he was a college student.

We danced several times after a nice dinner. As the bewitching hour approached, I began sweating out the "let's stop at my place for a nightcap" routine. I felt it coming and hoped he didn't have a place. Maybe it would never come up and I could get home, ending this evening with no hard feelings. Maybe he'd be the all-American boy type as I'd pegged him. This was the '80s when men no longer made the first move. Maybe he knew that. I sure wasn't making any moves, but I was conflicted too. I didn't want to go to his romper room, but I didn't want to hurt his feelings. My people-pleasing personality crept to the surface.

When he turned in a direction that didn't lead to my home, I knew I was destined for the confrontation I feared. My thoughts flashed to my teens—wrestling with out-of-control hormones in the back seat of a Chevy. *How did I get here? Oh, yeah, I wanted to feel young again.*

We pulled into the driveway of a fine suburban home complete with a swimming pool and an RV in the back yard. "Oh, I didn't expect my roommates to be home." I had a sneaking suspicion his "roommates" were his parents. He wanted me to believe this was a bachelor pad.

I could tell he hadn't counted on this turn of events. I figured the presence of his parents meant he would get me home where I wished I'd stayed that night. But he was quick.

"Why don't we have a nightcap in my rendezvous out back?" What he meant was a "little nip and roll" in the bunk bed over the cab of the RV.

I was in no mood to wrestle with Boy Toy. He had wined and dined me, but there had to be a way to say no without deflating his ego.

I'm worried about his feelings! What about my principles? I had yet to learn that straightforward, direct responses are best. The southern belle syndrome had gotten in my way, and I needed to mark my boundaries. I had learned how to play this game from watching Doris Day and Natalie Wood in the movies when I was young. I needed lessons on how to be clear about my expectations.

My mind raced backwards. Southern charm and sweetness had been my persona. Not wanting to hurt anyone's feelings and putting others before me invited close encounters of this kind. Here I was again, having just turned forty—I should have known better. I was backed into a corner, acting like an ostrich. I knew where this was headed—I just didn't want to face it. Obediently following him into the camper, my heart sank.

He babbled on about this being his quiet place next to the pool where he spent much of his time. Memories of college. I frantically tried to think how to end this.

Had I been so foolish to think he would want to take out an older divorced woman and get nothing for it? Someone must have told him that experience counts! Maybe he'd been with older women before and found them to be less inhibited than the sweet young things his own age. Whatever the reason, he clearly had the wrong idea about me. I felt guilty. Had I given him that impression?

I talked my way out of a disastrous evening with just a little arm wrestling. I was lucky that he responded to my firm, "No!"

Although that night ended fine, I wish I could say that was the last I saw of him. This young man was persistent. He ignored my words about not being interested and instead remembered my friendly body language when we met on the dance floor. This was the anything-goes '80s. My naiveté about the dating scene put me in jeopardy. He turned up the pressure valve to 380 degrees, calling me, asking me out, talking pleasantly on the phone.

Now I had a problem on my hands. When someone says, "Don't fool with Mother Nature," believe it!

He kept calling. I began to worry. I could sense an erratic nature. I had rejected him, and he didn't like it. His conversations became more persistent, provoking me into arguments just to connect. It became creepy.

I tried to be pleasant when he called, hoping he would grow tired of getting nowhere fast. But "niceness" was not the way to set boundaries in a situation that was becoming potentially dangerous. This took a while for me to learn.

Finally, he stopped calling. Thinking he'd grown weary of my evasive responses, I hoped his memory of me had faded.

I moved to a new home. Somehow he found my phone number. Could he find my address? What if he was watching me? The calls ended for good after I told him I was getting married. Even then I had to convince him it was true with several more calls.

We see through a glass dimly, then face to face. To me that night was just an arm-wrestling match. To him . . . I was entering his little black book forever.

In 1988, the year after I became blind, Jerry bought me a dog. Not just any dog—an Akita. Hundreds of years ago the Japanese emperor bred these dogs to protect the children. They were known for being quietly observant and extremely protective. An Akita does not bark when alerted to possible danger—it attacks. We named him Mikado and called him Mick. True to his breed, Mick loved children and people. If a stranger entered my house who Mick sensed was safe, he greeted him in a friendly manner and then ignored him. If he didn't trust someone, he stayed close to my side, ever watchful.

With Mick by my side I felt comfortable and safe, even living alone. In fact, so comfortable that on the night of my storytelling meeting, I unlocked the door early and put out a sign, "Come on in." I never gave a second thought to being blind and living alone. I trusted people.

A fireman called earlier in the week after reading my notice in the newspaper. He inquired about the meeting, adding that his friend was a budding story writer.

The meeting was scheduled to begin at half past seven, but the young couple arrived at seven. I was headed back down the hall for the great room when I encountered them. It unnerved me that Mick did not let me know I had guests in the house. I knew he always barked when friendly folks arrived—he loved the attention. But not this time. He did nothing to warn me that someone was in the house.

They took Mick's silence as approval and walked right in, not calling out to let me know they were entering. Were they shy? I suppose they were looking for me. I can't say if they were aware of my visual limitations, but so many articles had been written about me over the years that I often met people who already knew of me.

Rounding the corner, I almost ran into them. They quickly introduced themselves as the new visitors to the storytelling cluster group. Nervously, I invited them into the kitchen. So uncomfortable with their early arrival, I fidgeted with the new earrings a jeweler had just designed for me until I finally took them off and laid them on the counter. These treasured earrings were gone when the meeting was over.

A nice sized group arrived. Of course, I knew the rest of the storytellers. At the end, I mentioned I was working on my comedy routine for a class I was taking and needed someone to critique me. No one spoke up. I was surprised when the young fireman called the next morning offering to critique me. When I hesitated, he said, "My writer friend said she would like to help you, too." I relaxed. Not wanting to appear rude, I agreed.

The next day was overcast and damp. I had an uneasy feeling that I couldn't shake. The fireman called to say his girlfriend was moving and couldn't work out the time to join us. This made me uneasy. I started calling around looking for someone to be with me when he arrived. I talked a friend into coming, but she wasn't sure how early she could get to my house.

The day grew darker—in my mind, at least. I answered the door with trepidation, and the day became more dismal as he entered. This dark creature that had no face was saying something to me. I could only hear the clunk that hit the floor.

I jumped. "What was that?"

"It's only my briefcase. Did I startle you? I forget that you're blind."

I shuddered, feeling cold and wishing he would leave. My gut screamed this was wrong, yet I led him back to my office. Mick became my shadow.

As his briefcase clicked open, my imagination snapped to work. What was in that briefcase? What was he planning to take home in that briefcase? Not me, I hoped!

I asked again. He answered in a calm, quiet voice. "Just newspapers that might cultivate ideas."

Ideas for what? I envisioned little parts of me wrapped in those newspapers. My blood ran cold. *He was just a nice man who came to help me out. Yeah, right, Fiona, and you are the Queen of the Nile!*

His girlfriend was the storyteller, so I wondered why he was the one carrying newspapers to "cultivate ideas." My nerves went into overdrive.

I stammered about my friend who would arrive any minute. Trying to appear calm and collected, I turned to my computer to review my monologue. I was in no mood for my comedy routine. Then I heard him stand up and walk around the side of my desk to peer over my shoulder as I typed. I began pounding the keys. I felt his breath on my neck.

"What are you doing?" I demanded.

"Oh, you don't mind if I watch, do you? It's fascinating how you can use the keyboard without vision."

"Yes, I do mind. I have never liked anyone watching me type. Sit down!" I commanded in my teacher voice.

"Something wrong? Am I making you nervous?" He was needling me.

Nervous? Panic-stricken was more like it. I had to get him and his bloody briefcase out of my house. I bantered about the comedy event at the Punchline the next week, stalling and wondering why Sue hadn't arrived. I picked up the phone and called her. She said she'd be another hour. I couldn't stand the thought of being alone with this spooky guy for another hour!

I took a deep breath and said, "I hate to tell you this, but I've made a terrible mistake. I invited you over when actually I'm sick. I thought I was better, but my stomach is feeling worse. I must ask you to leave. I'm sorry you came for nothing."

I babbled that Sue was bringing me medicine and would be here any minute—anything to stall so I could think. I remembered my training as a teacher: When a conference is going badly, use body language and psychology. Stand up. Take command by moving toward the door as you close the meeting. I did exactly that. But he didn't budge. I stood at the door of my office, trying to appear authoritative.

Would I never learn that being blind makes me more vulnerable? Why was I so brave? I did not feel brave at the moment!

"Go ahead," he suggested as he clicked the briefcase. "I will follow you."

Oh, no, you don't. Brother, I am not turning my back on you. "No, I will wait," I said firmly. "It's best that you walk ahead. Mick is very protective, and I don't want to make him nervous."

I hoped that made him think twice. Never, never, never reveal just how afraid you are—even if you have a vicious Akita at your heels. Mick was there, silent as a lamb, but he never left my side.

The man allowed me to follow him out. Then he turned and stopped again in the foyer. He was saying something, but my heart was pounding too hard to hear. Holding my breath, I eased him towards the door. Clunk went that briefcase on the floor again. Would he never leave? Was he sizing me up? Was he casing the place? Was he intimidated by my dog or just amused? The big question, of course: Was he sinister? I don't know. If he was sincere, why did he never visit our cluster meetings again? I never saw him or his girlfriend at any storytelling event after that. But then, if he had come, how would I know? He might have been as silent as when he first entered my house. After what I call our "close encounter," he certainly wouldn't make a point to say hello.

Was this a lesson? Yes. I was too vulnerable to have meetings in my home.

Close encounters can be deadly.

And, yes, I am learning to trust my intuition more each day. I share these thoughts as a warning to others, especially disabled people. I do not have the answers.

Dr. Right once told me, "You are in a shower of firepower that's raging over your head—bullets flying and loud noises all around. If only you could step out of that foxhole and view yourself in the situation, you would be better able to see the potential for danger."

Wow! Aren't there times we all need to be more aware?

One more story to lighten the mood. It's definitely about a close encounter, but let's just say . . . of the furry kind.

After Jerry and I were divorced, I needed to start a new life. My son urged me to move closer to his family, so I moved into a small house a mile from them. It was another adventure. I liked the idea of being near the two grandsons and the new one on the way. They wanted me to babysit—like I was a sighted person! But I took to this idea like a duck takes to water.

The house in Duluth hadn't sold yet, but I moved anyway. I was unpacking on Saturday night, insisting on doing it alone. I didn't want to be a burden.

It was getting late, and I was starved. I had washed all the clothes, sheets, and towels. I threw the wash on the bed and walked back to the kitchen to rustle up some grub. The only thing I could figure out was peanut butter. *That's easy. I can smell it.* I grabbed the jar, took a long sniff. No odor. *Hmmm, must be my stuffy nose.* I took a spoon and scooped up some peanut butter using the back of the spoon. I'd heard this would make it easier for spreading. I covered one slice of bread and started to reach for another. *Oh, heck, I'll just make a roll up with one piece of bread.* I wasn't that hungry. I took a huge bite. Ugh! It was not peanut butter! I discovered I was about to make suntan cream my dinner.

I threw that out and took some popcorn to bed.

In Cold Blood was the movie that night. I settled in under the warm quilt, really getting into the movie—just the dialogue, of course—so I began folding the laundry to stay awake.

I'm not sure when I dozed off, but I awoke with a start! Something crawled across my quilt-clad toes and jumped across the bed, towards my head. I sat bolt upright to reach for the phone. The hair on my neck prickled up. *Call Chance. My son will rescue me!*

Whatever it was jumped and knocked the phone out of my hand. I was dancing, trying to slip into my bedroom shoes. Running out the door with the TV screen crackling in the background, I grabbed the door behind me and heard a bang as the creature hurled itself against the door.

Phew! I think it's trapped inside. I'm safe!

I scurried to the great room and sat. *Think, Fiona.* I didn't want to sound like a baby. I wasn't afraid of the dark. After a few moments, I got up and put on the kettle for tea. Once the tea was made, I sat and sipped and thought.

Then . . . a rattling of bags or so it sounded. I jumped and frantically dialed my son. "Chance, this house is full of hairy, scary creatures. Please hurry."

My daughter-in-law, Rebecca, opened the door. I stood petrified like wood, still as a statue in my pink pajamas and robe with a phone in one hand and my cane in the other. I knew I was "treed." The disgusting critter was circling my legs.

Rebecca burst out laughing. "It's a possum! No, it isn't. It's a f-f-f-ferret."

"What's a ferret?"

She told me.

"Where's Chance?"

"Oh, he sent me instead. I'm the hunter in the family."

I didn't wait for an invitation. I was in her car in a flash. I wasn't sleeping there until they figured out how that ferret got in my house. I gladly waited in the car while Rebecca returned him to his rightful owners next door, shuddering as I thought about the slinky, creepy mink-like fur ball who shared my bed that night.

Every day is a new adventure.

15

Live at the N.F.B.

In the year after my divorce from Jerry, twelve years after becoming blind, I made my first trip without a sighted guide to The Cavett Institute in Arizona for professional training as a speaker. I applied for a guide dog and produced a successful benefit show for Canine Vision. I was invited to join the board of the Georgia Chapter of the National Speakers Association.

I was doing everything to take my mind off the divorce. Nothing new. That is the way I deal with loss. Forge ahead. Don't think about the sadness.

A young woman who worked for me found the Convention of the National Federation of the Blind (NFB) online. NFB is an organization of proactive people who are visually impaired. She suggested I check it out.

I was intrigued. I had been acting like Super Blind Person, cape and all, as if I needed no help from my peers. Now I needed to explore this group to find out what other blind people were like . . . to learn how they coped and lived.

The convention would be in Atlanta in July, so I registered. What an eye-opening experience it turned out to be.

I made a reservation at the Hilton, because the Marriott, where the convention would be held, was booked. Staying at the Hilton would mean crossing the street with my cane. I admit I was scared, nervous, even petrified, but ready to meet the challenge. Although the Center for the Visually Impaired had trained me for mobility, I hadn't used this training much yet, because I usually traveled with someone.

Five thousand visually impaired people were expected to descend on Atlanta that week, many with guide dogs. I wondered how the event organizers and hotel employees would handle all those dogs going to potty. I'm sure they wondered, too.

To prepare, I planned for several friends to take turns assisting me. I convinced them it would be an enlightening experience for them as well as me. Some found the exhibition a bit overwhelming, because the signs were in Braille on the fronts of tables rather than eye level. The blind people could read the Braille signs with their hands, but my sighted friends couldn't find their way around. Lots of feeling and touching going on.

Guide dogs sniffed each other. Canes found a thrill or two. The event featured wall-to-wall sunglasses and canes. Many people linked arms to keep up with each other. One vendor gave out cricket snappers to click for people to find each other. They didn't work in a crowd of blind folks, though—too many crickets clicking. The chirping reminded me of the Okefenokee Swamp of my childhood.

My friend, Cathy, was with me the day Tommy, my computer guru, showed us around. Tommy knew the ropes. He could talk computer lingo with the tech geeks in the exhibition hall, and he had enough sight to walk without a cane, which was useful. I was grateful Tommy could guide us to the vendors with the latest technology.

Like a big kid in a candy store, I went through the vendors' section drooling over all the blind aids. I wanted to touch every table. I wanted to buy it all. I bought an iron corn muffin pan with a device for pouring without spilling. It cost $25.00. You have to really want to cook to buy a contraption like that. It wasn't as easy to use as I thought it would be, so I gave it away to my namesake, Fiona Leanne, who is a great cook. She loves it.

A Braille Scrabble game looked like fun. I bought it, even though the grandchildren weren't old enough to spell. I bought a picture book by Bill Cosby to read to the boys and a volleyball with a beeper inside. I wanted a voice organizer, but the voice sounded too robotic and cost too much. No way!

The highlight of the convention was an attraction called the Touch Safari that featured stuffed or simulated animals available for touching. My friend Clyde was so impressed with it that he insisted on picking up my family members and bringing them down for the experience. My grandson James was only five, and Camden was three. They loved it, and so did I. I felt some incredible animals—the mammoth and the snake were the most interesting. The Touch Safari was the topic of my grandchildren's conversation for months.

On the third day I anxiously waited for Jane and Sheryl to show up. I couldn't imagine why they were late. When they did not arrive in time to escort me to the next session, I ventured out alone, not that I wanted to. I certainly was not accustomed to finding my way through a sea of dogs and canes, but I was determined to get to each session before the doors closed.

My friends finally found me seated in the session where they were supposed to escort me. They arrived, apologetic, saying, "Fiona, we would walk a few steps, and someone would stop us and ask for directions. We couldn't get here any faster. We couldn't refuse them." The hotel clearly did not have enough volunteers for the event.

• • •

Later Jane and I headed to the elevator. She whispered, "There's a good-looking guy with a guide dog coming our way."

Excited, I said, "Yeah?"

"Do you want to meet him?"

"Sure," I said.

His named was Steve. I wanted to know what he looked like, so I reached out to touch him. Luckily I found Steve's forearm and not another body part. I had been known to make that mistake. Touching him told me his shape and size. He wasn't hairy; he was smooth. We chatted and made plans to meet at the next session.

Jane dropped me off at the session and left, but then it dawned on me—how do two blind people find each other in a crowd? If only we both had a talking GPS! I never could figure out where he was.

Back in my room I remembered that I knew his name. I could call the front desk and ring his room. I dialed Steve and invited him up. Flash! *Oh, my, what have I done? What if he gets the wrong idea? I don't know how much sight he has. Could he corner me? Could he overpower me?* I just wanted to make a friend. It didn't hurt that he was cute.

Steve knocked on my door. I invited him in and gave him a tour of the room which was silly of me. His room probably looked and felt the same. We both sat and got acquainted. It was awkward at best. He didn't stay long but promised we would talk again later. At the door, I impulsively hugged him. *Why did I do that?* I guess I wanted to "see" what he looked like. The lack of eye contact and body language make it tough to connect. I never ran into him again the entire weekend. I lost his phone number, and that was that. How many opportunities do blind people lose?

I know I was bold, but how else could I meet anybody? I wondered how I looked, like that was important—he couldn't *see* me. He wouldn't know if my makeup was smeared or my hair was mussed, but he sure would know if I had bad breath.

I believe sighted people often are more relaxed around me, because they know I can't see them. I wonder if other people who are blind feel isolated like I do sometimes.

People at the NFB seemed eager to network. Most convention goers came in groups and knew each other. The people who made new friends were the talkative ones, like those who grouped around vendors.

I invited Joe, a high school boyfriend who had surfaced after my divorce from Jerry, to be my sighted guide on Saturday. I also invited my friends B.J. and Fred to join us at the dance that night. B.J. asked me, "How are these people going to meet and greet at the dance?"

"I have no idea, B.J. I guess we'll find out."

When we entered the ballroom, the band was playing "We're Having a Party," a '50s song by Sam Cooke, but no one was dancing. The band was rocking and the beer was cold—and free. I was glad to have a sighted date who could lead me to the dance floor.

Joe said, "Let's get the party moving," as he grabbed my hand. It was a big crowd to move—several hundred people. I had forgotten what a great dancer Joe was. He put on a show for those who could see. A buzz hummed around the room. We ignited the party by playing social directors, introducing people to each other. Each time we headed to the dance floor, we bumped into people and shouted, "It's party time . . . come on . . . let's shake a leg!" I could feel the energy shift.

One young woman was moving to the music, ready to rock 'n' roll. Fred started up a conversation. At first she thought he was hitting on her. She didn't realize he was trying to fix her up with the blind musician at the next table. By the end of the evening, Fred was pleased with himself, because he could see those two were in the clinches.

I left hoping the sighted volunteers helped the beer-soaked conventioneers back to their rooms. Lying in bed that night, I thought about how thankful I was of my new assistant's persistence. Her gentle encouragement was the impetus I needed to seize this opportunity to meet other blind and visually impaired folks. I had been living in a small pond the past twelve years. My days were spent telling stories and giving speeches such as "Autograph Your Life with Purpose" and "Embracing Change—Even When It Isn't the Change You Want." The admiration I received from my sighted friends for my courage to live blind and stay involved with my craft spurred me on. I thought I was doing well. However, the four days I spent meeting my peers who seemed to effortlessly navigate a new city and connect with each other made me realize that I was not nearly as brave as they. The convention goers I met simply amazed me.

After a weekend of being around the leaders and followers of the NFB, I returned home feeling empowered. I vowed to stretch my limits and step into new experiences without a sighted guide or assistant—to seek a new kind of independence. A real independence.

16

Just Another Blind Date

The doorbell rang. Palms sweating, I ambled toward the foyer. It isn't easy to be chic and sophisticated when one cannot see.

Harry rang again. I felt for the door, wondering how to tell my date that he needed to do an inspection of my appearance before we left for dinner. I had not met Harry before tonight, but I knew he'd been in the military, so maybe he was prepared for this.

"Hi, Harry."

He stepped in and said hello back.

"Do you mind being my fashion sergeant?"

"I would if I could see you."

Of course . . . the lights. He needed light to see. Too nervous to think, it never dawned on me that I hadn't turned on a single light in my house. I flicked the switch.

Hoping Harry wouldn't be too flustered, I leaned my head to one side and smiled. "How's my mascara? Is my slip showing? Do I match?"

"No," he replied. "I gave up smoking when I left the service."

"Huh?" I asked. I repeated my questions. After another false start, Harry admitted he was a little hard of hearing. He thought I'd asked for a match.

Great! I thought. *He can't hear, and I can't see! Hope we can communicate in the trenches . . . I mean the clinches.*

Arriving at the restaurant, it occurred to me that I should demonstrate how to help a blind person through a doorway. Giving Harry the quick version of sighted guide technique, we must have looked like we were doing the tango when we stepped through the door.

He escorted me to my seat and put his hand on the back of the chair. I slid my hand down his arm, finding the chair without incident. Waiting for our order, I assured Harry about escorting me to the restroom. "I can handle finding my way once I get inside." As for cutting my meat, I said that would be very chivalrous of him.

When our meal arrived, Harry leaned forward to tell me what food was where on my plate.

The waitress jumped in. "Honey, ain't you ever seen shrimp before? You must be from the Midwest or someplace like that."

I blurted out, "No, I'm blind."

Embarrassed, she began stumbling all over herself with apologies. (Why do people do that? It wasn't her fault I couldn't see.)

While I was thinking her embarrassment might get me a free dessert, she turned to Harry and asked in a loud voice if I might want coffee with my meal. I was amused that she suddenly felt I couldn't answer such a question myself. She turned back to me, trying to make conversation. "Sweetie, I bet you can read sign language."

"No, but I'm thinking of taking it up in case I meet a nice deaf man." She must have been a little deaf herself. She ignored my attempt at humor.

The waitress continued speaking loudly to be sure I heard her. Good thing, since Harry was hard of hearing. *Hmmm. If only I could get her to direct that shrill voice to the right affliction.*

I surmised she was a blonde. We Southerners have a saying, "Her cornbread ain't quite done!" It *is* politically correct to remark about your own species, isn't it? I am a blonde.

We managed the meal smoothly right through to dessert, which wasn't free.

The night was young, and it was Super Bowl Sunday, so we continued our evening at the nightclub next door. They were handing out test tubes filled with samples of Jägermeister licorice liqueur. I love black licorice candy. Thinking the liqueur was like that and they were free (or so I thought) I took one in each hand. "Yummy! I never pass up a free test tube." Drinking more than one or two glasses was not my style, but the liqueurs were easing the tension of a blind date. Harry began to "look" better and better as I downed three more. Wow! I felt as free as a bird.

Harry suggested we dance, and I was ready to swing. Turning around quickly, I reached out in mid-air and my hands accidentally landed on his behind. This saucy move might have thrilled Harry. Only it wasn't Harry—it was a woman's husband who had just stood up behind me. Not knowing I couldn't see, she moved in for a confrontation. Poor Harry was in the way and almost got the brunt of a potential pocketbook fight. But he saved the day, or night, as he gallantly swept me onto the crowded dance floor.

I love to dance the Carolina shag, but when we found space they began playing "Macho Man." I wiggled to the rock 'n' roll freestyle. The liqueurs had relaxed me enough to abandon my insecurity about holding hands to dance. I let Harry lead, oblivious to the world around me. To anyone who has never seen a blind lush dancing, it could not have been a pretty sight.

Twirling, I wound up facing the tables. I began dancing with a chair instead of my date. I felt a tap on my shoulder. Thinking someone wanted to cut in, I ignored the tapping. Still wiggling to the music, I exhibited my dancing prowess to the chair in front of me as Harry kept trying to get my attention. He tapped my right shoulder, then my left. I was rocking with the band.

Finally, they took a break. We returned to our table, but Harry seemed annoyed. "Why didn't you turn around?"

"What do you mean? We were dancing freestyle."

"I'm not accustomed to dancing with someone's backside."

It's a good thing I didn't let that remark spoil my evening. The night was young, and I could dance . . . even with a chair. What the heck! I was having fun.

Harry waited until we left to gripe more about my choice of dance partners. The wooden, straight back one, that is. Harry was embarrassed, and I didn't want to admit I was too.

I considered sharing my thoughts but decided humor was better. I made jokes about being blind.

"Mmm, Mr. Straight Back. Was he cute? Or a little too stiff?"

Where's your sense of humor, Harry? Maybe you're the one who's stiff.

The cool night air slapped me in the face and perked me up. I hadn't been called an independent woman in a dependent body for nothing.

Feeling cocky enough to think I could find the car door without his help, I darted ahead. This would have been my chance to see how much of a gentleman Harry was, but no, I had to show off my blind confidence. I wound up sitting on the dashboard instead of the seat. Thank goodness it was a convertible or I might have gotten a real zinger on my forehead.

We drove away in silence. You could cut the air with a butter knife. My dating future was hanging in the balance. Could this man handle the unexpected adventures of dating a blind woman? Was Harry thinking I was an exhibitionist? He probably thought I was a show-off, drawing attention to myself on the dance floor. I wanted to help him loosen up and see the funny side of life.

As we drove, I suggested he consider my assets. I was a cheap date, wasn't I?

"The Jägermeister cost $4.00 a pop. Would you like to know how many you drank?"

"No!"

I added, "But vacations would be a bargain. Sprinkle a little sand on my toes, stick a conch shell in my ear, and put me in front of a fan. I'll think I'm in the Caribbean."

I thought of another one. "Harry, you know that leisure suit leftover from the '70s that's hanging in your closet? You could get it out and wear it. It would always look fashionable to me."

No comment from Harry, but I was on a roll.

"You could look at other women! How would I know?"

Still silence from the driver's seat. I couldn't resist one more. "Think of all the money you would save on your electric bills."

"Besides, if it doesn't work out, you can tell your mother, 'She was just another blind date.'"

17

Airport Runaway

Before becoming blind, I could count my flying trips on one hand—Hawaii, San Francisco, Memphis, British Columbia, and Paris. These were the places I was lucky enough to see. I cannot count the number of times I have flown blind. It never gets easier.

My ideal trip to the airport would be to arrive in a limo, be transported in a golf cart complete with margaritas, then sashayed off to my private jet. Maybe one day when I sell enough books. For now I take MARTA, the mass transit system in Atlanta, like the rest of the little people in my city.

No place on earth feels more dangerous to me than the MARTA station. If I should step in the wrong direction I won't just fall twelve feet and risk breaking my legs—I will fall into a mass of electrically charged tracks that will give me a lethal jolt of reality when I land. Just think—if no sighted person had ever described that vision to me, I might never have known how dangerous the darkness could be!

Getting on or off the train without losing my coattails, or luggage, scares the stew out of me. Agility is essential.

• • •

I had been blind eleven years when I got my first guide dog, Sierra, a golden retriever. I needed to be more independent since I no longer had a husband. Having a guide dog would be a new challenge and provide a buffer for my loneliness. Of course, my new dog and I needed special training together in the places I would go in my normal routine, such as visits to schools for storytelling jobs and the MARTA station and airport for speaking engagements.

Unfortunately, my new dog had endured a frightening runaway incident on her way to my home for the first time. She was in a car accident in which the car ran away without a driver. I convinced the trainers to let me have her despite this. I wanted to give her a chance. She never really recovered from that trauma, though, so I had a nervous guide dog from the beginning.

A mobility instructor took Sierra and me on our first "test drive" through MARTA stations and the airport. I swiped my card and entered like a pro. Sierra found the elevator with no problem, and we descended to the train platform. Good practice. True, the trainer was watching from behind as Sierra and I made it this far alone. Next, I was instructed to find the stairs. Graduation time! I needed to prove to my trainer that Sierra and I had it down pat.

One little hitch—a guide dog doesn't know where to go any more than a car does. It was up to me to give her the right cues. How does a blind person do this? Ask for directions! (Some men would never make it.)

At this particular station, I had forgotten about the three flights of stairs with landings between each one. We had practiced a few times at other stations, but each one is laid out differently.

Sierra paused at the top stair, as she was trained to do. But when we finished the first flight down, the crowd of people and the fascinating scents penetrating her doggie nose became distractions. She paused again for refreshment. It could have been spearmint gum. Who knows?

I interpreted this as the end of the line—no more steps. To Sierra it only meant, *I think this is a good place for a sniff break*. Naturally, I paused with her, and then I urged her on with a slight jerk on the lead. My trainer had told me to reach with my foot for the edge of the steps before proceeding. Did I listen? No! I was totally unaware that steps leading downward loomed ahead. The trainer was no longer right behind us but separated by a throng of hurried travelers.

Sierra wouldn't budge. I jiggled the lead once more, assuming she was misbehaving again. I needed more experience to understand her moves. Suddenly, Sierra snapped back to attention to let me know there were more steps. The crowd was pressing in on me, so I urged her forward. With all her power, Sierra lunged. An observant man climbing on the opposite side must have been watching. As I began to tumble forward, he grabbed me in mid-air from across the banister. My heart leaped as I imagined what would have happened. If not for this stranger, I'd be lying at the bottom of those steps. Shaking, all I could do was mutter a weak "Thanks." The crowd moved swiftly on. I wondered if anyone else had noticed.

We ended the training for that day and returned home. Sierra and I needed several more sessions to be ready for traveling to the airport. Eventually, we did graduate. Since then, Sierra and I have made numerous trips with and without sighted guides.

Here's another quirk of Sierra's to give you a mental image of my airport runaway dog. She prefers to jump when traveling downward on an escalator—at least the last five steps. I have become quite proficient at jumping in mid-air with her. We must look like leaping lizards.

Air travel for a blind person is like maneuvering through an angry crowd in a dense forest. You feel alienated, vulnerable, violated, and humiliated. The journey can be stressful for any traveler, but for me it's like a safari with the heat and pressure—but no scenery! The lines are long, and the length of the walk at Atlanta's Hartsfield-Jackson Airport approaches eternity. Navigating through the airport feels like being shoved into a sack, then dragging fifty pounds of wobbly marbles behind.

The security system is a tunnel to me. I am "manhandled" through the little box with my computer, purse, and plane ticket stripped from my possession. I feel most vulnerable at this juncture.

When I travel with a sighted guide—a human being, that is—I must remember I'm at the mercy of a new person who is learning to direct me with their voice amid the clamor of the busy terminal. Getting me on an escalator without incident is a feat in itself. "Just put my hand on the rail," I request politely. Some remember, some forget. It's always a surprise.

I carry a backpack with a computer, transformers, rechargers, batteries, and a mini-disc recorder, plus a wobbly bag that cannot make up its mind which direction to roll. I call it the Black Monster, Wicked Witch of the West. She rolls catawampus and falls over like a drunken fool. She pulls on my weak shoulders and rips my elbow out of joint. She once caused me to walk into a giant pillar of concrete. The concussion put me in bed for two days. Oh, how I vow to throw this black beast into the gutter and walk away! But each time I get home my frugality sets in, I cannot bear to throw it away and buy a new one. Until the next trip, I forget how naughty that suitcase can be.

For me, the highlight of any airport is the restroom. If my escort is a man, I must maneuver alone through the angular opening to the ladies' room, tapping my cane across the marble floor to the twenty stalls. Which one will be empty? Tap, tap, tap, bump the door, finger the latch, and determine whether it swings in or out. It really takes a mathematical mind.

On my first blind adventure in an airport restroom, I cringed as my fingers traced the stall. People assume handicapped stalls were designed for all disabled people. Not the visually impaired—narrow stalls are much easier to navigate. Try it yourself. Close your eyes and touch the unsanitary walls until you find that porcelain throne! Then hover over it, balancing your elbows on your knees. It is quite a feat—one I have mastered, I'm proud to say.

Next there's the toilet paper that usually comes in enormous rolls, so they will never run out. Unfortunately, they're wound so tight that each patron is awarded only one thin square, unless it's a well-used roll. New rolls mean the first six patrons must claw their way through the first inch of tissue. Panic-stricken that I will be searching in my purse for a used Kleenex or worse, be forced to use my slip, I always wonder how much time I have left to get a wad from one of those tightly wound rolls before losing my balance in this ridiculous position.

The first time I used the airport toilet, I waved my fanny over the bowl and heard a loud whoosh. I quickly pulled up my underwear and said, "Excuse me. I didn't know this stall was taken." No one had thought to tell me that restrooms were now equipped with automatic flushers.

Imagine my surprise the first time I reached for the water faucet handle and heard it turn on by itself. I always say, "Thank you," just in case.

My biggest surprise was when I rushed into the restroom at an airport restaurant. It had a gift shop selling many Southern items, including oak toilet seats which were also used in the restrooms. I didn't spare much time to look on my way to the john. I flipped up my skirt, urgently relieving myself of the water I'd taken in during the last hour, only to discover that the restaurant was displaying their lovely oak toilet seat with the lid down inside the restroom! Imagine my chagrin when I felt my left shoe fill up.

On the airplane, we are packed in like sardines and my dog shivers like she will go into convulsions and throw up at any minute. It is torture!

The plane is so noisy that working on the computer or listening to a book is difficult. It bugs me that I don't have facial clues to determine if the person next to me wants to talk or to ignore me. Sometimes I wonder if they are interested in meeting me but are uneasy about taking the initiative. The tough thing is, if I am not traveling with my guide dog or displaying my cane, they don't know I can't see.

One time I decided I would be bubbly and cute and even try to fake out the guy sitting next to the window—about my blindness. I was dog-less that trip. He was busy working on his computer and probably didn't want to be bothered. I pretended to be a sighted passenger, chattering like a myna bird, totally unaware of his preoccupation. He barked, "You are interrupting my work." I apologized and explained that I didn't know he was busy, because I couldn't see. I wanted to slide away in embarrassment. He was aghast. For the rest of the flight, he tried to make up for his rudeness. I just wanted that flight to end.

My brother-in-law loves to come to the airport to pick me up. He says when he is unable to find me in a crowd he cocks his head to one side to listen for my shrill voice telling a story to a fellow traveler. If that doesn't work, he looks for an animated blonde with the cell phone to her ear, waving with the other hand, perched on the same kind of carry-on bag that everyone else uses. I gesture wildly and wear black to catch his attention as I keep talking. It works every time. At the luggage carousel, he patiently tries to identify my common black luggage. I insist that I have made it easy this time—I have tied a satin ribbon around the handle.

"What color is the ribbon?" he asks, dryly.

"How should I know?"

18

A Very Dirty Little Story

Clyde Cawley got up to stretch his long legs on a flight from Atlanta to Buffalo, New York. He stopped where I was seated and asked, "Don't I know you? Aren't you Fiona Page?"

I couldn't recognize him with these sightless eyes. We conversed for a minute before I realized we had met at the Georgia Chapter of the National Speakers Association two months earlier. Clyde went back to his seat to retrieve a copy of the book he'd just written, *Cancer, the Gift of Life*. He handed the book to the stranger seated next to me and asked, "Why don't you read this to her?"

The gracious woman agreed. She read to me from that book until the plane landed at the Buffalo airport.

That's how Clyde and I became fast friends. From that day forward he coached me on planning and conducting seminars. He also introduced me to the editor of his book, Marcia West, who has been invaluable to me with this one.

• • •

Clyde accompanied me to the University of Georgia for our second presentation of the month. "Embracing Change—When It Isn't the Change You Want" had been well received. I had my mentor to thank for that, and I was looking forward to presenting with him again. This was to be the largest seminar that I had conducted to date—a half-day program for the Georgia Department of Juvenile Justice.

As we discussed the program on our two-hour drive from Atlanta to Athens, I told Clyde I wasn't happy with the story I had planned for the program's "worst day" activity. I had plenty of them, but not one that seemed funny enough or even significant other than the day I woke up blind. Who could top that? My bad days somehow just seemed to be a blur. I wanted to share an *ooh, aah, ha ha* day! I was drawing a blank.

Sierra, my guide dog, happened to be traveling with us. This was her first overnighter. At one point, Clyde remarked, "She's so thin. I don't think I've ever seen a golden retriever so skinny!"

I assured him I had fed her the required two cups a day for a working dog.

When we arrived at the hotel, Clyde took our bags and helped me get settled before going on to his room. He opened Sierra's bag of dry food and asked if he could feed her.

"Remember, Clyde, only one cup per meal," I said.

He protested. "She looks so hungry."

"She's always hungry. She would eat the table if she could."

I heard him pour the food into the bowl and wondered—was Clyde listening to me? I suspected not.

Later that evening Clyde and I attended a dinner dance with Sierra in tow. People at our table were intrigued. "She's beautiful," they said. "Let us hold her leash while you and Clyde dance."

I politely declined and tied her to my chair as I glided onto the dance floor on the arm of my friend. "Being given treats like that teaches her to beg," I said while we danced. "That's a big no-no for guide dogs. It breaks their training."

Then I heard something.

"Clyde, I think we're surrounded," I said, turning my face up to my tall friend.

"What do you mean?"

"Aren't you noticing how popular we are? It isn't us! It's Sierra! We are surrounded by dog lovers! I bet you she is enjoying a feast despite my protests."

When we returned to the hotel at eleven o'clock, Clyde offered to take Sierra out to "potty."

"No, I think we should go together." We walked down the block in the warm spring air. Sierra had no interest in the concrete. She wanted her grassy backyard. We tried for ten minutes to get her to relieve herself, but she wouldn't go.

"Maybe she'll be all right until morning. She's been like this before in new places," I rationalized.

Settling in for the night, I hoped Sierra could wait.

This hotel was an older building. My fourth floor room was not far from the lone elevator but that didn't help at all. It was so slow you could brush your teeth while waiting for it to arrive at your floor. The place for Sierra to relieve herself was a whole block away. All I could do was pray she would make it through the night.

I awoke in a sweat in the wee hours of the morning from a nightmare of my college days. Loud music, pushy, intoxicated people, and the cops beating on the door, I felt the pressure of obnoxious party animals trying to drag me out of bed. It was only Sierra's cold nose poking me on the shoulder. Her whimpering told the story. This was urgent . . . now she wanted to go.

"Oh, no, Sierra, I'm not sure I can find the elevator! Why didn't you go when we took you out?"

It was far too early to disturb Clyde, so I put Sierra in the bathroom where the tile floor was cool. *Stay calm.* Just a little bit longer. She had been known to wait as long as nine or ten hours when necessary. I was hoping she could do it this time, but if she couldn't, I reasoned that at least it would be easier to clean up a tile floor than carpet.

Now unable to sleep, I opened my computer to check my notes for the seminar. Sierra was restless. Every time I heard her stir, I prayed a little harder, thinking, *Please, please wait, Sierra—just a little bit longer.*

Sierra began scratching and whimpering desperately at the bathroom door. I checked my watch and it was only 4:35 a.m. I decided perhaps if I went into the bathroom to do my makeup that might calm her down. I certainly wasn't going to let her back into the bedroom. If she was going to have an accident, it had to be in that tiny bathroom.

As I stood at the sink, talking softly to her, I noticed Sierra becoming more and more agitated.

Then I heard a loud "splat!" A horrendous, malodorous smell filled the tiny bathroom.

Oh, no! What was I to do? I couldn't move. I was standing barefooted in my pink satin pajamas. My long trouser legs dragged on the floor.

I was wedged between the toilet and the counter.

Toilet paper! I grabbed several squares and let them float down to the pile of brown custard until I had the huge mound gift wrapped in tissue. I gingerly cupped the stinky mess in my palms and edged over to the toilet. "Aha! Almost there!"

As I reached over to the toilet bowl I remembered that I had put down the lid to keep jewelry from falling in. Assuming a Chinese contortionist position, I wriggled my toes under the rim of the lid and edged it up. Just as I dropped Sierra's surprise package, the lid started to fall causing my aim to be slightly off. Ugh! I scraped it up and gasped for air. *Whew—it's in!* I quickly flushed.

A scary thought hit me the moment my fingers released the lever. Harvey, my brother-in-law, had lectured me many times. "Too much tissue combined with poop will clog the plumbing."

Too late! The water level was rising, and my feet were getting wet. The overflow was headed for the carpeted bedroom. Sierra and I were still trapped in the tiny bathroom. She was whining. I wanted to whine, too.

I grabbed the doorknob and leaped over the stream of murky water to the carpet with Sierra right behind.

I hurriedly felt my way to the bedside phone and called the front desk. A woman answered.

"Ma'am," I said, "I don't know what time it is, but I hope you haven't had breakfast yet. I'm about to tell you a disgusting story."

Catching my breath, I unfolded the whole ordeal into the phone. The woman didn't laugh. I went on to explain that I needed a plunger, some disinfectant, and some help . . . *quick*.

I checked my watch. It was 5:30. I didn't want to call Clyde and wake him yet since we didn't need to be at the event until 8:00. I still had time. My head was scrambled, but I counted the hours until I had to go to work. I had to eat. I had to feel better, and I had to do a good job today.

Maybe I should have some breakfast and try to relax, I told myself. I called the desk clerk back and said, "I understand the maintenance man is on his way up, but would you mind ordering me some breakfast? I'd like some grits, eggs, bacon, toast, an extra carafe of coffee, orange juice, and some cinnamon rolls."

After a long pause, the clerk said, "Lady, you're not really going to eat at a time like this, at least not in that room, are you?"

"On second thought, I guess not. Send it to Room 406!"

Then I hung up the phone and went out to the hallway to wait for my hero—the maintenance man.

Before I could turn, the door clicked behind me. I was locked out in my pajamas! Sierra was on the other side of the door. Now what?

In due time the elevator opened, and my rescuer appeared.

"I am so embarrassed," I stammered. "I wish I could clean this up instead of making you do it."

"Lady, I've seen a whole lot worse than this during football season. This is University of Georgia territory."

I couldn't imagine anything worse.

"Oh, my gosh! I've got to warn Clyde that breakfast is arriving in his room." I dialed quickly to explain the dilemma.

"Why didn't you wake me? I'd have taken her out," he chastised.

"It was too early to bother you."

While my knight in shining armor was cleaning up, Clyde appeared at the door to rescue me from the stinky room. I handed Clyde my suit.

"Let me go get your shoes and briefcase," he said.

"Not now!" I demanded, grabbing his arm. "I want to get out of these soggy pants."

"That's the best offer I've heard yet," he chortled.

I ignored his comment. "We've got breakfast coming."

"Breakfast?"

"Yes. Can you imagine what the desk clerk will tell her friends today?"

Clyde chuckled all the way back to his room.

Breakfast arrived. All Clyde could say was, "How can you have an appetite at a time like this?"

"I've already heard that once today. You forget—I didn't see it!"

"But you smelled it."

"That I did!"

"Just think. Now I have a better story for the example of my 'worst day' ever."

As I stood on the stage telling the story, I could sense that Sierra kept standing up.

I noticed this and remarked, "My loyal guide dog knows this is her story."

It didn't take long to figure out that was not the case.

Clyde came onto the stage and whispered, "Sierra and I are taking a walk."

19

A Valentine Wish

Keeping my third grandchild every day while his parents worked was a joy. Still, I was only fifty-eight years old. I wanted to dance again. Be out there playing with people my own age.

Well, this would be a first! I had never been to a singles dance in my life, much less a formal one. I can tell you I was nervous, but determined to get there. I wore a black and silver evening gown and black strappy satin dancing slippers. And I came home with the "Hot Lips Valentine" balloon—a gift from the cool guy who sold tickets at the door.

Venturing alone into the world of dancing was a new experience for me since becoming blind—one that was uncomfortable, to say the least. Truth be told, I was scared to death. But I thought if I didn't go through with it I would never know if I could be attractive to another man again because of my handicap.

As I walked in on the arm of my thirty-year-old son, the ticket man whispered, "Go, girl! Save a dance for me!" How could he know what encouraging words those were?

I had struggled all afternoon, discussing with Chance just how I was going to get to this dance and who would bring me home. Being the caring son he is, he protested. "Mom, I don't like you going without a ride home established ahead of time." He sounded like he was talking to a teenager.

"I don't care. Don't you see I have to go even if it means getting a room at the hotel where the dance is being held? How will I ever know if someone would take out a blind woman? I can't meet anyone as a couch potato." I just knew I had to do this.

We finally worked it out. He would drive me there and my new girlfriend, Jennie, would give me a ride home.

That evening on the way to the dance lots of questions crossed my mind. I wondered how I would make eye contact to meet someone to dance with. Just how would I connect, being blind? I wasn't sure how I was going to handle this situation.

Jennie had arranged to meet me at the dance. She called ahead to alert the ticket man that a blind woman with blonde hair would arrive around eight o'clock and need help being seated. Plans were set. I didn't need to be afraid of anything, but I was shivering in my boots . . . dancing slippers, that is.

This sweet ticket man glided me around the perimeter of the dance floor. It was a night for Cinderella. Grateful that this man was so sensitive to my apprehension, I moved about the room with confidence. Still too self-conscious to use my cane for mobility, I took the arm of my prince when the music stopped. I had made it through the first dance. I giggled. "I will show you how to be a sighted guide."

"Great." He grinned, I imagined.

I took his arm just above the elbow, and when we got to the chair I suggested he put the same hand on the back of the chair. He complied, and I slid my hand down his arm with grace. I hope I smiled. I had made it inside the dance hall and to my chair.

Jennie found me and started bringing guys over to meet me. Dolly, the owner of this great singles club, made sure my table was reserved and came by to speak with me several times. I suspect she also invited men to ask me to dance.

The atmosphere was sizzling—not much drinking and no smoking, so I was in Seventh Heaven. The place was packed with many people in their fifties and sixties. The ratio was about even as to men and women, which was surprising. Jennie strategically placed me next to the Kisses for Sale booth. I was sitting between the DJ and the Kisses—a good place to be! I danced with Terry, Kevin, Larry, Roy, Bill, Jim, and Bill again. No kidding, I was like a teenager at a sock hop. I memorized those names as they came up and asked. I lost count. I never dreamed I would have a chance to dance so much.

One partner actually made me believe in chemistry without eye contact. When he touched me, I imagined how he looked. I felt the electricity between us and wondered if he felt it, too. Never dawned on me it could be the wool and nylon we were wearing. Could he possibly be my dream man? Feeling a strong attraction but unsure of what he was feeling, I kept the conversation going long enough to learn he was a college professor. This bright man was quiet and unassuming and had done interesting things in his life. He modestly told me about designing an Internet service provider. Someone told me later it was a well-known company.

I think he was curious about me, too. We had a lot in common—we were both in the teaching profession, had traveled to some of the same places, and enjoyed similar interests. I was worried about monopolizing his time, so I made a remark to give him an opening to leave. Unable to read his body language, I assumed he was just being nice. I never got to "see" him again. When Jennie came up, I whispered, "Jennie, where is he?" She told me that he stood in the back of the room alone for another hour, then left.

Why did I do that? My insecurity blew it for me once again. The Heavens shouted: Let go and let God. If it is meant to be, that is not for me to decide. I needed to keep reminding myself of this. I had read in one of those books written by another visually impaired person that it was courteous to give people an out, so they would not feel stuck babysitting someone who is blind.

When several men danced with me, they asked if I wanted to know what they looked like. *How odd.* It seemed important to them that I know how they look. Women rarely ask. Maybe it's just an icebreaker for the men. I did notice that dressing up seemed to bring out the chivalry in men. I was enjoying it, and so were they.

Soon I realized that "scent" was going to be my identifier of the male species. Many men would ask me to dance and not mention their names. As I tried to figure out if I had danced with them before, it became apparent that I would have to bone up on my aftershaves. Let's see, was he Polo or Old Spice? No, I think the man of my dreams was Cool Water.

The men were as scared to dance with this blind woman as I was scared to dance with them. *Take a deep breath and be glad you're dancing, Fiona.*

I discovered that with Women's Liberation, men didn't think they had to walk you back to the table. I worried that I might be stranded. That meant I had to let my dance partner know each time about my visual problem. I also needed a strategy for my escort to direct me to my seat so I wouldn't look like a blundering idiot.

Awkwardly, I suggested, "Touch the back of the chair and I will follow your lead."

I tried to think of clever things to say about being blind like, "Look into my eyes, Sweetie, the lights may be out, but I'm still home!"

"It sure is dim in here, isn't it?"

"Honey, my radar is working tonight. Is yours?"

Women of the new millennium stood to chat and cruise the men's faces and moves, talking to whomever, with one eye on the available men out there, staking out a man to ask to dance. The ones who remain sitting act as if they are invisible, as if to say, "I am not here, you gorgeous hunk, that is, unless you spot me. Then I will act like I'm here for the picking."

How could I compete? *I can just see me cruising! I'll have to get a lot better with my nose.* When all that aftershave mingles with all the perfume, my sense of smell fails me. If only I could figure out how to flirt!

One man squeezed me slightly as he remarked, "Don't worry, I'll take care of you." I nearly melted—for the moment. Beware of those caregiver types. They can get nasty when they're not in control.

After three dances, Joel, an acquaintance from the speakers association, led me to the table, thanking me for the dance. As he walked away, I reached with precision for my glass, only to have someone politely take it from me. I looked in the direction of the arm and smiled. I thought it was Jennie playing with me. A female voice suggested that I slide over and make room for her friends. Oblivious to the possibility that I might have been placed at a different table from my own, I retorted, "I can't move over. There's no room."

She nudged me and insisted, "Perhaps you're at the wrong table."

Astonished, I wondered if that could be true. I couldn't believe it. I was confident this was my table. Surely Joel wouldn't sit me in the wrong place!

I pointed out to the woman that this was a reserved table—reserved for Fiona Page, and I was Fiona. For reassurance, I calmly reached for the basket of Valentine candy that Jennie had brought to mark our table. It wasn't there! But I still couldn't believe I could be at the wrong table.

Icicles dripped from her words. "This is our table."

I stated again, more firmly, "Oh, no, this table is reserved."

I pointed in the direction of the sign that wasn't there. "See, this says, 'Reserved for Fiona Page.'" As I reached into thin air for the imaginary sign, my confidence deflated quickly.

She wasn't going to give up. "This is our table."

The hens were backing up and scratching, marking their territories. "I'm sorry, but you're mistaken," I said, again reaching—I hoped—for Jennie's basket of Valentine candy for assurance as I stood my ground once again. Where was that darn basket!

Slowly, the truth sunk in.

"Oops. I am so sorry! I am blind, and I guess you girls cannot tell. That gentleman sat me at the wrong table."

They were shocked. Switching to a syrupy sweet voice, one asked, "Can we help you find your table?"

Find my table? Even *I* didn't know how to find my table. Then I remembered the candy. "Yes, look for the candy!"

That broke the ice. As it turned out, my table was the next one over. Now we laughed when guys came up and stuck their hand out to gesture for a dance, then turned away grumbling, wondering why I rudely ignored them. My newfound women friends joined in watching the quizzical looks from the guys and describing them to me. Jennie joined us to explain to the men who were so confused. Some were appalled at the idea of dancing with a blind person and slinked away. I kept up my tough exterior, not letting it bother me.

I made friends with those ladies, probably because I could laugh about the embarrassment. It wasn't easy. What other choice did I have?

As we closed down the place, dancing the last dance and my balloon trailing behind me, I wanted it to last forever just like my sixteenth birthday dance. The night ended with me wondering if this was the place to meet Mr. Right. It certainly was fun in the meantime.

I will return next year.

Happy Valentine's Day!

20

Behind the Glitz and Glamour

After my second divorce I moved to a small, comfortable ranch house a mile from my son and his family. I was delighted to discover that one of my neighbors was Avis Fox, an acquaintance through my storytelling circle.

I didn't know her well, but I was fascinated that she was seventy, sophisticated, and genuine. Avis was a svelte, attractive blonde. Our conversations told me she led a glamorous life—making commercials, acting in small cameo roles on television, and modeling for magazines.

I was envious. When I was forty, I had taken acting classes and pursued a talent agency. I wanted to be in commercials. Family life took precedence. That dream faded.

Avis often walked between my house and the next as she made her daily trek to the creek bed that ran through my property. One spring day, Avis joined my friend, Kathleen, and me as we talked in my front yard. Kathleen had seen the photo and article in the newspaper about Avis being crowned Ms. Senior Georgia. She congratulated her.

My former next-door neighbor from my previous neighborhood also had been crowned Ms. Senior Georgia. I found that ironic, and it gave me an idea.

"Do you think I could be in the Ms. Senior Georgia pageant?" I asked timidly. The words came out of my mouth and surprised even me. I was fifty-nine years old at the time, just six months away from becoming eligible.

Avis was gracious as she petted Greta, my guide dog, "Well, I don't know why not. Do you think you could walk across the stage alone?"

I didn't know the answer, but I quipped, "Where there's a will, there's a way." After she left, I began to wonder. *What's gotten into me? How could I pull off all that a pageant entails?*

I began to reminisce about the Miss Southeast Georgia Bathing Beauty title I won when I was seventeen. But that was in 1960—I was now forty-two years older—and blind.

The next day, Avis came back with her scrapbook and shared the entire experience of winning the Ms. Senior Georgia title and going on for the national crown.

I was transfixed. Immediately I called my friend, Marcia, and said, "You and I are going to see the Ms. Senior Georgia pageant." I didn't know what to expect—what was a senior citizens' pageant like? I expected it to be a lot different from my teenage pageant where the outcome was based almost entirely on physical appearance. I would have to "see" it through my friend's eyes.

I have to take a minute here to share with you a funny tidbit about my grandson, Camden. When he was three, he plundered in my closet and found that trophy. A Miss America statue was atop the trophy. He asked, "Whose trophy with the Cinderella on top?" he had just received his own trophy for soccer. Now how do you explain that to a three-year-old? I mused, "Well, I won the bathing beauty competition when I was seventeen."

Camden expressed surprise, "You mean you just standed up there and showed your beauty?"

Later I called the director, Connie Rosenthal. Unable to reach her by phone for months, I was sure it was a conspiracy to avoid this blind woman who thought she wanted to be in a beauty pageant. It turned out to be nothing like that. When we finally connected, I was amazed at how she pulled off such a pageant. She and her staff made me feel right at home.

At the pre-pageant workshop, the co-director, Carla, placed a CD in my hand. "I noticed that your computer talks to you, so I made this CD with the schedules and all the instructions you need to enter. It's the first time I've ever done this, so I hope it works for you."

That meant so much. Now I didn't feel like I was operating in the dark. I would be informed like everyone else. At the workshop that day, I realized I had much preparation. The biggest obstacle was keeping up with communication. The ladies talked, but they also used their facial expressions and body language—I depended on words.

It helped to have a girlfriend close by to stay connected with the activities. The other contestants were surprised I was able to keep up with the dance number. They didn't know I had been dancing all my life—before and after becoming blind.

But dancing was the least of my worries. My pride got in the way. I tried to demonstrate how self-sufficient I was without offending the other contestants. Gloria wanted to hold on to me like I was a two-year-old. It didn't take her long to see how independent I was which created another problem—how and when should she offer assistance. Since I wasn't comfortable with asking for help, we were at a stalemate. It would take time for us to find a comfort level.

I emailed all my girlfriends and asked for help. Marie volunteered to make a poodle skirt for my comedy routine, "Just Another Blind Date," a throwback to the '50s. It's based on the story I described in my chapter by the same name in this book. Elayne was enthusiastic about being my makeup artist. Cathy and Shirley volunteered to assist with anything I needed. Jane and Gerda came forward with shopping for costumes and jewelry—and the generous sponsorship.

I never thought about winning. That seemed like an impossible hurdle. I only wanted to meet the challenge of feeling free, confident, and able to be independent. I wanted to be able to select the right wardrobe. I wanted to be able to handle the quick costume changes. And I wanted to be able to use my mobility skills effectively on the stage. I knew mobility was the weak link in my armor. This pageant was just the incentive I needed to overcome that weakness.

During the months leading up to the pageant, I wondered how I would pull off looking like I knew what I was doing. Suddenly a mirror was important to me. Friends always turn out to be the best mirrors anyone can have.

Keeping up with jewelry, shoes that matched, several changes of clothing, and all the rules of the pageant was like being on Broadway with no experience. I could fall flat on my face. But I didn't allow myself to believe that would happen to me. I just wanted to have fun, make new friends, and be able to say that I did it.

The pageant started with a Thursday evening dinner for all the contestants and officials. Each woman shared a compelling story about the adversity in her life. This was the night to bond as sisters. I thought I had been through a lot until I listened to these brave women. For example, Barbara, the contestant who spoke before me, had overcome breast cancer and a recent stroke, yet she was an accomplished dancer who was several years older than me. *How did I come to be in such outstanding company?*

On Saturday the excitement was contagious. I was nervous, but Barrett, the stage manager, leaned over and whispered, "You go, Frisky!"

I stood in the wings, waiting for my Marine escort to walk me on to the stage. Those two made me giggle which helped me to relax.

"Just Another Blind Date" rocked the audience. I had attended Jeff Justice's comedy class and developed a funny piece about being on a blind date. Avis helped me polish it for the pageant. I got high marks in my interview with the judges. With my family and friends cheering me on and my Goddaughter, Maggie, and Camden yelling at the top of their lungs each time I walked on stage, I knew it didn't matter whether I won or not. I was having a blast and reaching the goals I had set for myself.

That night I floated home on laughter and applause.

On the third day, when they announced the winner, "Ms. Senior Georgia 2004," I was stunned—they were calling my name! Like in a dream, I took the arm of my handsome Marine escort and stepped out to the front. Someone lifted my guide dog, Greta, onto the stage. She crawled under my turquoise gown and peeked out at the audience.

The spectacular night ended in exhaustion. Hardly able to move the next morning, I awoke thinking about my victory. *Now I'm a Queen, and I don't know what to do.* By noon, the phone was ringing off the hook. The newspaper wanted a quote. My hometown paper called, too, and Jerrye, our social director, phoned to explain my queenly duties.

The following year was full of pomp and circumstance. I had to learn to wear more makeup, dress in glitter and gold, and always wear my baldric (sash), which told my claim to fame. I could feel the purple and white magnetic signs for the doors of each chariot in which I rode. And, oh, how I loved riding in the parades. People in the crowds picked up on my name because of Princess Fiona in *Shrek*. I wanted to pinch myself to be sure this thrill was all mine. I had been teased about wanting to be the center of attention, and now I was.

. . .

For the next six months we prepared for the national pageant to be held in Biloxi, Mississippi. Being a contestant in the Ms. American Classic Woman pageant was the highlight of my reign. I was overwhelmed by the fuss over me, the fabulous wardrobe, and all the high heels and jewelry showered on me for the national pageant. Connie and Margaret made me a new costume for my comedy routine—a pink felt poodle skirt with a sophisticated black poodle in a rhinestone collar and leash. My '50s saddle oxfords were painted a glittery gold. My top was made of black jersey knit with a sequined pink "F" to represent Fiona. I wore a clip-on blonde pony tail.

My family and ten of my friends came to cheer me on. I felt blessed to have so many supporters there. I felt like royalty.

I won first runner-up and was so proud to have my ninety-three-year-old mother in the front row, cheering me on, thanks to my sister and brother-in-law, who made sure she got to be a special part of this event. That meant so much. With all the pressure off, I danced, laughed, and sat on the arm of my mother's electric wheelchair while she whirled around like she was dancing, too. You may remember this scene from "Freedom of Choice," which serves as a tribute chapter to my mother. She had as good a time that night as I did.

We talked about the winner's rendition of Patsy Cline's "Crazy." She was a gorgeous six foot tall blonde. It was an honor to be named second place to such a doll.

Alas, the clock struck the fateful hour, and Cinderella had to retire her golden slippers. The following spring I relinquished my crown to Ms. Senior Georgia 2005. For this event I dressed as the Queen of the Nile in a shimmering turquoise jeweled costume. I was carried out to the stage on a spectacular lift by my muscular "slaves." My entire family was there cheering me on as I belly danced my way to the end of my reign.

My grown nephew, Anthony, teased me as we celebrated that evening. "You looked splendid, being carried out by your Egyptian slaves. That is . . . until you stepped off your platform. I was in the front row ogling your two belly buttons, one with a jewel in it."

"What do you mean two?"

Anthony poked me in the arm. "Remember your little pit left over from your heart surgery?"

I gasped! But I had a comeback. "I should have stuck a jewel in that one, too."

"Old" queens are soon forgotten. My crown lost its glow, but I kept the memories. Would I have entered a pageant such as this, if I had never become blind?

Probably not.

All pageant contestants are invited to join the Georgia Classic Club. This sisterhood exceeded my expectations with its worthy purpose to inspire and entertain. We travel wherever we're invited under the name, The Dazzling Dames. We perform for conferences and civic clubs—any organization that wants to be entertained. We encourage other women over sixty to live life to the fullest in service to others. Each year members of this group visit more than one hundred senior centers, assisted living homes, retirement communities, and nursing homes. The ladies' talents range from singing and dancing to acting. I am always spellbound by the Hollywood atmosphere.

I think it took awhile for my Classic Club sisters to get accustomed to my self-deprecating humor. I had to show them how to help me pick up on cues for being on stage and to get comfortable with being my sighted guides. They learned how to help me maneuver the steps, the chairs, and the buffet table. These vivacious, outgoing, gorgeous gals were warm and willing!

• • •

I have been asked many, many times, "How do you get yourself ready without any help?"

As queen, I had plenty of help. Now several years later, donning my sash and dripping with glitter, I join the gals once a year for the pageant. But, more than the glitz and glamour, I'm excited by my growth in an important area for me—learning to get ready on my own.

I still agonize over having to prepare for such events. *What if I choose the wrong outfit, mess up my makeup, or can't find the things I need?*

As a sighted person I was able to bathe, wash my hair, get dressed, and be out the door in thirty minutes. Of course, sometimes I applied makeup while driving. Now I apply makeup while my driver is driving.

I often wake up early worrying about how much there is to do when I need to get ready for an event that requires additional preparation, such as a pageant. At first, I felt like I was slow as a snail. I prayed for the ability to get dressed quickly like I did when I could see.

After twenty-three years, I've trained myself to again be ready in thirty minutes—hair-washing and all. I admit it can be tricky. Obstacles, such as cabinet doors which I forget to close, dropping things, rushing around, and even smearing mascara all slow me down.

I have developed some techniques. I lie on the bed and breathe slowly while applying mascara. Yes, it takes a steady hand, a good memory, and organization. It requires so much focus. Concentration and planning are imperative if I want to avoid a catastrophe.

If I don't know my driver, I have to depend on my own careful efforts to get that makeup on without mistakes. Ultimately, I'm still never sure if I have been heavy-handed with it.

My friend, Marie, says, "You move as though there are no obstacles in your way. You surely move by faith alone—sighted people don't walk that fast even in their own house."

How many times have I been in such a hurry that I wore mismatched shoes? A board meeting, an attorney/client meeting, Toastmasters, storytelling engagements—too many to list. Once I stepped to the floor at a singles' dance wearing one suede bottom dance shoe and another tap shoe. They felt the same on the top. Oops! Forgot to check the soles. The music was loud, but I could feel the step of one shoe and the tap of the other. I hoped no one could tell that I was step, tapping to a swing number. After the song, a gal stopped me to ask where I learned clogging.

Keeping up with the time is twice as hard when you live alone and can't see. I have a talking watch and a singing clock. Little things can go wrong. Dropping an earring on the floor can cost me another five minutes. If it rolls out of my immediate reach, my motto is "leave it."

A lesson that life continually reinforces is this: Nobody listens carefully enough. This applies to me too. But, when I need help, I have developed tricks to capture someone's attention like changing my voice.

Another lesson I keep re-learning as I grow older: A smile goes a long way.

When I sit in my house and want to have the freedom to do something, I know a taxicab is the only way. I have to be cautious, trust my driver, and plan my trip carefully. I may need to make several stops like lunch, the bank, the cleaners, and then off to my grandchildren's school to tell stories. I often wonder how other blind people manage their lives. I continue to be grateful for God's angels on my shoulders.

21

Cooking Capers

Fall is the season for cultivating. I get restless. My desire for accomplishing something overtakes me, so I set about thinking of some self-improvement scheme. One year I had bought sanding equipment to refinish old furniture like I did when I could see. Then it was to save money. This time I wanted to see if I could do that again.

Actually, this sense of restlessness was not only confined to the fall season. After my reign in 2004 as Ms. Senior Georgia, I felt I had nothing to look forward to. Living alone was boring until my grandson Ethan got home from pre-K. His four-year-old energy kept me busy until his parents picked him up in the evening. All through pre-K and kindergarten he had helped me cook.

Now it was 2007. I came up with a new endeavor. I set out to spend my mornings improving my cooking skills.

Step One: Call the Center for the Visually Impaired. I had not talked to my counselor, Nell, in many years. I wondered if she would remember me. When she answered the phone, I explained how I wanted to try cooking again. My end of the conversation went something like this:

"Yes, I had a brief class—maybe three or four weeks. No, I couldn't cook well when I could see. I am too impatient. Even my ex-husband reminded me of the time I substituted catsup for tomato sauce. It was quicker than running to the store. That was in my sighted years. My family has made fun of my spaghetti ever since that day."

I was sure she remembered how impatient I was about learning Braille. That story about me cheating at Braille likely had circulated throughout CVI. Nell was kind enough to avoid the subject as she probed for more information about my skills.

"My first training was two months after I lost my sight. Vocational rehab sent out a sweet, tiny lady. She put Braille dots on my electric stove and told me I would be safer using gas. It could be turned off quickly. My family disagreed about me being around an open flame, so I kept the electric stove."

That seemed to satisfy her, so she switched back to what lessons I had learned.

"What kinds of things did we do? Well, let's see, she taught me how to pour liquid with my eyes shut," I said, deadpan. Silence on the other end of the line. "Just kidding! I didn't need to shut my eyes. I spilt it with no problem at all."

Fortunately, she had a good sense of humor.

"We talked about labeling, but I must have been very adamant about my distaste for cooking and grocery shopping. I think she was frustrated and gave up but I didn't give up. I tried a few years ago when another cooking commander came to the house. We basically talked about labeling canned goods, and she brought me some long quilted oven mitts. She went on maternity leave, so I didn't see her any more. I think I tend to distract my instructors, and they don't come back!"

My counselor ended the conversation with, "I hope you're eating well."

"Oh, yes, my six-year-old grandson has been helping me since he was three."

She asked my goal.

"I don't really know. I think I want to cook one decent meal before I die."

Nell had just the right instructor for me. She would send her to my house three times, so I could learn to prepare that one decent meal.

"One thing is for sure. My grandchildren will grow up without fear of spilling things. It's a regular thing at my house, and it's usually Grandma Fiona doing it!"

From the time they could talk, Ethan and Helen would say, "Here, Nene, let me do it for you!"

My counselor said she had to see these grandchildren for herself. She planned a visit to my house to discuss our plans.

Step Two: Make a good impression on the new cooking instructor. Before she arrived, I had banana bread mix in a bowl, peas in a pot, and boiling water ready for the bag of brown rice. I wanted her to see how capable I was. No sense in wasting time. I wanted to get to the root of my problem.

I could only imagine her reaction to observing all this clutter in my kitchen. When she first arrived, she was quiet. That made me nervous. When I get nervous, I talk. A lot.

The instructor finally spoke, "I don't think I have ever seen one of my visually impaired clients multi-task quite like you do."

She seemed thoughtful and then had an idea.

"It's much easier to have a systematic approach. Why not place a tray on the counter for the tools you will need, and tackle one dish at a time," she said.

I don't think I was listening. I was mixing up the banana bread while explaining that my boiling bag of rice always stuck to the pot.

My counselor pressed on. "You need to be more methodical in your efforts."

Right then, I secretly named her Attila the Hun. This was going to be a long day. It became a chant with her saying, "Slow down!"

I wondered if she looked like her new nickname. She explained with increased patience what each number meant on the dials on the electric stove.

No wonder I burned so many pots.

When I was a young wife, stovetop dials had only high, medium, low, and simmer. This one had 10-9-8-7-6 . . .

On her third visit, my instructor announced, "You're ready to sauté chicken." I imagined a drum roll. She showed me how to prod the raw meat. She talked me through the task, using my fingers. When she got to the ring finger, I shouted, "Ring man. Pinky means it's done!"

We practiced this over and over. Probing with a fork did not feel like the end of my finger, but I smiled and complied.

"You'll get the hang of it," she assured me, as she packed to leave.

Nuts. Crockpot cooking sounded like a great idea.

Exhausted, I was pleased that I had sautéed the chicken. I assured her I could finish alone. I had given all the patience I could muster to getting that chicken cooked thoroughly. Elbow deep in mixing up wine-laced chicken pot pie, you would have thought I was birthing my first child.

Step Three: Serve my masterpiece. I purchased the highest quality chicken I could find at Whole Foods, determined to serve this grand meal to my son and his family that very night. For once I would not hear, "Mom, what's this thing floating in the soup!"

The phone rang, jarring me out of my daydream. My daughter-in-law was on the line. "Rebecca, how does a gourmet dish of chicken pot pie with wine sauce sound for your dinner?" I quickly added that my cooking instructor had helped with this creation, so Rebecca would not disappoint me and turn down the offer.

Tired from a long work day, a supper that was ready sounded good to her. I had thirty minutes to finish it up in the oven.

Ethan set the oven to preheat. I had Braille markings on the oven's flat screen, because I had not mastered the digital timer. Sometimes my fingers aimed wrong, causing the temperature to be either too high or too low. I wasn't taking any chances for that to happen. I opened the crescent dinner rolls to show Ethan how to separate them. "We will place these on top for the crust."

A quick flash ran through my mind—sloshy liquid. *I need a cookie sheet under the casserole dish.*

I donned the bulky oven mitts. With my gloved left hand I opened the oven. Steam rushed to my face. The pot pie teetered on the cookie sheet in my right hand, and began to slide.

I hadn't thought this through.

Ethan stood on a short stool right beside me, playing with the left-over dough. I'm sure he heard my gasp.

Like a small child sailing down a sliding board head first, the pot pie headed straight into the oven ahead of the cookie sheet. I scrambled to achieve some leverage with the aluminum sheet.

Too late. The pot pie tilted as it bumped the rim of the cookie sheet and spilled out into the bottom of the oven.

Ethan and I were stunned as the delicious aroma showered the oven with its creamy mixture.

Ethan cried, "Oh, Nene, I should have been watching!"

Trying to retrieve some of the expensive food, I laughed—when I wanted to cry. "What a mass of soupy mess! Oh, it's not your fault, Ethan, sweetheart. It was just a careless accident."

We figured out how to save the day . . . or at least some of the meal by retrieving about a third of the mixture and making more dough. I told Ethan, "Sometimes I mess up, but you must not feel that it's your fault. We just have to make the best of a bad situation. We'll still have our chicken pot pie for dinner."

My young grandson takes his job seriously and does it well—always watching to give me advice, to be my eyes, or to read directions to me.

I chirped with confidence, "Looks like I've got enough to make a meal out of it. This will be our little secret, though."

"Okay, Nene."

"Now hand me a can of mushroom soup." My cans are well-organized, but we were on a time crunch.

We repaired the disaster by spreading a little Bisquick over the top. My estimate was off, and I needed just a tad more. There had been a crescent roll left over. I knew that Ethan had been playing with it, but his hands were clean. "Hand me that last roll, Ethan."

"Oh, Nene, I am so sorry! I got it wet and threw it in the trash!"

"Oh, no!" I said without thinking. I knew there was no Bisquick left either.

Ethan burst into tears. "I'm so sorry." He muttered his apology over and over.

I grabbed him and gave him a floury hug, whispering, "Don't cry, Sweetie. If anybody needs to cry, it's me for dumping our supper into the oven."

We both protested whose fault it was. Then we began to giggle. And giggle some more.

When Ethan left to go home with his makeshift casserole for his family, he called out to me, "Remember, Nene, don't use the self-cleaning part of the oven. You know what happened the last time—the fire truck came. Nene! I will come this weekend and spend the night with you, and we will use the self-clean together."

I pondered the previous two hours. We did manage to save enough for the Page family to have a delicious dinner.

• • •

Thinking about the mess to clean up, I lost my appetite and decided I would just drink my dinner in my easy chair in front of the TV.

You'd think that would be simple, but, no, it wasn't. I grabbed a bottle of wine from the wine rack, thinking it was a screw top bottle. *I'm not fighting with a corkscrew tonight.* In fact, no point bothering with a wine glass either. A juice glass would do.

I poured a half glass and gulped it down. Surprise! It was not wine. It was the expensive berry juice I take for my antioxidant each day. Now I was more than healthy and covered in soupy mixture, so I peeled off my jeans and sweater, dropped them in the washer, and dragged myself to my bedroom.

As I crossed the foyer, I felt a cool breeze. Ethan had run out the door without closing it. What an end to a frustrating afternoon. I streaked to my bedroom! *Who cares what neighbor is watching!*

I may be impatient, but I don't give up easily. A year later I got acquainted with Chef Jeff and engaged him for more culinary education. I must say he's been the most help of any one of my instructors. He knows about food and utensils and cooking times. I now have much more confidence in the kitchen. I can braise, sauté, and cook really good vegetables. I haven't burnt anything in a long time. I am eating quick, healthy, fresh foods. No Lean Cuisine for me! In fact, my next book may be a cookbook for the impatient.

22

I Hope You Dance

When I first heard Lee Ann Womack's song, I was intrigued by the lyrics. What a magnificent message about living! It said to me, don't sit on the sidelines—participate in life. Breathe, feel, smell, taste, and touch—be joyous. People need to stay connected. We give each other energy and encouragement to live well. I certainly developed my love for people through dancing. It keeps me young and revitalized.

This book was initially called *Dancing in the Dark* because when I sat down to write these stories, I realized that much of my life centered around music and dance. My grandparents (whom you will read about in the second section of this book) had square dancing parlor parties in the same living room where I grew up listening to "The Green Hornet" on the radio. When I was in seventh grade Daddy converted our front porch into a dance floor. Well, some of my best memories are of dancing on that shiny yellow pine floor. He wanted his girls to enjoy dancing. My parents were smart cookies—they provided a place for my sister and me to socialize. I was the only thirteen-year-old who had dance parties. My girlfriends and I would sit on the floor snuggled up against our boyfriends, and eat popcorn while playing games like Spin the Bottle.

My parents kept the tradition of dance going when they opened the Dari Kream and added "Teen Town" in the back. Daddy really knew how to build a great dance floor. When I wasn't working in the front selling soft ice cream and hamburgers, I was begging Daddy to give me a quarter for the bright royal blue and gold jukebox in "Teen Town." Daddy would wink and smile as he gave me a break to dance.

Daddy met Mama plugging nickels into a jukebox in 1939. I met my first husband at a matinee dance. For years we had parties, dancing to the latest tunes. I remember "Proud Mary." It was Motown time.

At forty, I had the dance fever again. I met "blue eyes" (Jerry) on the dance floor. As relationships go, we got settled into a routine and gave up dancing for "eating out"—not nearly as much fun! Dancing is much healthier for you. I whined, but it didn't do any good—Jerry gave up dancing. I didn't want to give it up.

After I became blind, I spent so much time concentrating on learning how to do tasks that were once effortless, such as walking into new places and threading a needle, that I found myself wanting to do something as effortless as it always was. Something that didn't require much adapting or learning new skills. One day my counselor at CVI asked, "What do you want to learn to do again?"

My eyes sparkled. Dance was the first thing that sprung into my mind. "I want to dance again," I said. "Could I dance—blind?"

"Of course you can." She asked me a lot of questions about where Jerry and I used to dance. I told her Studebaker's was our favorite hotspot. Soon the plan was mapped out and I started my mobility instruction on dancing. That night we met at the '50s era dance club just outside of Atlanta. She arranged to get us in early to practice my mobility before the crowd arrived. I was jittery. I was going to be the only blind person in the place. I had to practice and count the steps to the restroom, to my table, to the dance floor. Suddenly the place became crowded. Wall to wall people—where to put my hands? How could I keep from knocking over a drink or poking someone in the eye? Thankfully, Jerry was there with our friends to smooth the way. I felt so happy and alive. Dancing was the answer to what I craved.

I discovered dancing gave me a new sense of freedom. It reminded me of how in the first few months after becoming blind, I had begged Jerry to take me to the beach so I could run into his arms on the sand. That's freedom. It made me feel normal and forget all that I had endured the last few months.

Unfortunately, Jerry and I could not make our marriage work. Years later I was again wishing I could dance. I tried dance aerobics. That didn't work. My classmates had to take turns getting me back in my place. I often wandered into theirs.

Inspired by the lyrics of "I Hope You Dance," I auditioned for the National Storyteller of the Year competition. I was first runner-up to the 2000 Storyteller of the Year. You may be wondering what that had to do with dancing. Isn't it about participating? Joining in? Sending in my audition tape for that competition meant I had to walk with confidence onto a stage with my guide dog. I say that is the same joy as getting out there and dancing. It all requires poise and balance.

Dancing was my daily diet. A doctor once told me, "Keep up the dancing, Fiona, and you will be forever young. You will keep your ability to walk, to balance, and not fall."

When my new grandson, Ethan, arrived and needed a babysitter, I began keeping him daily for four years. He went everywhere with me—even to my storytelling gigs. I had to have balance to walk around with that little bundle of joy.

Then one Friday night, exhausted from childcare, I lay on the bed and said to myself, "Life is passing me by. I have always loved to dance. Why am I not out there?"

Another voice answered, "You're blind! How will you make eye contact? How will you know when someone is asking you to dance? They might not even ask—you may be a wallflower. Can your pride handle that?"

"If I can just get one person to ask me to dance, they will see I know my way around the dance floor," I argued with that little voice.

My good angel nudged me, "You're going to need a friend for this. Go for it!"

Dance fever struck again. I threw my slipper into the ring!

But you have already read that story, "A Valentine Wish."

After that Valentine's Day I was determined to continue to dance. My friend, Sue, mentioned a 40+ singles dance at the Holiday Inn. I offered to pay the way if she would go. She is both pretty and gregarious. She could gather a crowd of men. Sounded like I might get to pick up a few crumbs. Just kidding—I only wanted to dance again. Yes, it was awkward at first, but the music stirred me to move.

The crowd was friendly. Soon I had a circle of acquaintances that saved me a seat and watched out for me. Guys didn't know I was blind until they asked me to dance. Then they were stuck with me! I proved I could hold my own on the dance floor. They often asked me again. Some were not good dancers, but they were nice people.

Some nights I might not know how I would get home but I knew I had friends. One was Bob, who became my buddy and my safety patrol. Whenever Bob was there, he asked me if I had a ride home or if I wanted a drink. He was a great dancer, too. His hawk eyes scanned the dance floor to keep up with me. If he saw me walking around with a man looking perplexed, he swooped in to guide us back to my seat.

One night my son dropped me off at a costume ball. I wore my stage costume for the Ms. Senior Georgia pageant. I was certain I would win wearing that cute little pink skirt with a black poodle with a rhinestone choker collar. I got out of the car and twirled around for my two grandsons, "How do I look?"

"Cool, Nene," they said in unison.

When I got home that night, I was mortified. I had the skirt on wrong side out! The pink poodle with the rhinestone chain didn't show! No wonder I didn't win! So much for asking for the Page boys' opinions!

One Friday when I had been "out there" for a couple of months, a friendly guy came up and asked in a New York brogue, "Let's dance, Sweetie."

I asked his name and misunderstood. "Bernie?"

"No," he said, "Ernie, as in Bert and Ernie!" I thought he was a little silly, but I accepted another dance. Fast songs were his idea of fun. At first it felt weird for our arms to be jerking up and down to the music. I had never heard of the Lindy Hop, a dance that caught on when Lindberg made his famous trans-Atlantic flight.

Ernie had learned the Latin dances when he was stationed in Puerto Rico in the service. He had fantastic rhythm and was an amazing lead. As we became friends, he kidded me about keeping up with him. His chiding spurred me to make it my challenge. "Mambo No. 5" became "our song." I knew to be ready as he switched from cha-cha to mambo to merengue to try to trip me up. I stayed right with him, getting my workout for the evening.

One day while getting my nails done I overheard the lady in the chair next to me talking about dancing. We struck up a conversation. I overheard her say she went to dance places alone. Immediately my brain flashed, *potential dance buddy*. In five minutes we had made plans for Friday night.

When Leigh picked me up, I showed her how to be a sighted guide. As I took her arm, I could feel that she was petite. She had already hinted that she was older than me, but she was dressed in youthful leggings and high heels. We sat there for a while, getting to know each other. I wasn't getting to dance as much as I usually did. I leaned over to Leigh when the DJ announced Ladies' Choice, sighing, "Every time the DJ makes that announcement I get the urge to ask a guy to dance."

My new friend whispered in her throaty voice, "Honey, all you have to do is stand up slowly, turn to the right, then ask the tall, handsome man who just came in. He's right behind your chair!"

I stood up, turned, smiled, and reached up because she said he was tall. My hand brushed his cheek—I got his attention. "Do you dance?" I asked, not realizing I sort of slapped him.

He recovered quickly by taking my hand and said, "Sure."

On the way out to the floor, I stopped, pulled him towards me and whispered, "I'm blind. Is that okay?"

"You can dance, can't you?" he replied.

I laughed as he twirled me around. Chuck was the best swing dancer I had ever held onto. We swung to Sam Cook and did a little rumba to several other songs. Then the DJ played, "In the Still of the Night," a slow song from the '50s. By that time, I thought he might want to shed me and find another partner. I pulled away. With a deep voice he leaned over and asked, "Where are you sitting?"

"I don't know, you've got me all turned around, but I can always count on my friend, Bob, with his hawk eyes. He is short, bald, and always in a white oxford shirt—he will know."

Sure enough, Bob came to the rescue.

Now I did not want to give up this great Fred Astaire that I had just found. At the next dance I asked Ernie if he knew Chuck. He did. Whenever Ernie and I were together, I asked, "Is he here?" Ernie loved to take the opportunity to play matchmaker. He was sly and would ask me to dance, then motion to Chuck to come take over. As Ernie led me onto the floor, he and Chuck would switch off. When I turned around, I would be in my new guy's arms. They made that switch so fast and smooth that it became a game with them.

Chuck waited six months before he asked me out. I willed it to happen. Each time we danced, the chemistry was electric. I just dreaded the day he would ask me how old I was. I was convinced that he was much younger than me. I had never lied about my age. I wanted to now! As it turned out, I was wrong. Chuck was a gentleman; he never asked. We dated for six months, then decided being friends was the best idea. We have remained dancing friends ever since.

I hope to dance 'til I die.

23

Dialog in the Dark

One evening I was at a party listening intently to my German friend, Gerda, as she described a venue that enthralled her on her recent visit back home. "It was a pitch black warehouse separated into five sections: a park, a marketplace, a busy street, a boat ride, and a restaurant. Each area was a simulation of the real thing. Upon arrival, you were placed in a small group, given a white cane, and asked to proceed into the dark arena. Each group was led by a visually impaired tour guide."

"Fiona, I went away having a better understanding of what it's like for you."

I was fascinated by this innovative enterprise. I began imagining what company I could interest in bringing Dialog in the Dark to America. Coca Cola? Disney? I envisioned it as an exhibit for single parents looking for something new to do with their children on the weekends. As a storyteller and former teacher I felt I could market the idea to schools and become the educational liaison. I had heard the Sci-Fi Museum had financial woes, so I made an appointment to meet with the director to pitch my idea. I thought my Christa McAuliffe

Fellowship credentials and the science museum named in her honor would give me an in. He was polite but not interested.

Three years later I heard on the radio that a Dialog in the Dark exhibit was opening in Atlanta—the first city in the U.S. to host this venue. Wanting to be on the bandwagon, I called the director full of ideas of how I could fit in. Already overwhelmed with her new job, she suggested I come to the next informational meeting. I engaged my friend Rhonda as my driver and joined the masses of potential tour guides—one hundred blind and visually impaired people vying for a position.

My plan was to try to talk with the person in charge of hiring. "Maybe this could open the doors for more storytelling gigs," I told Rhonda.

When we arrived I was immediately swept up into a large, crowded hall with instructions to complete an application to be a tour guide. I didn't want to be a tour guide. I wanted to be their spokesperson. "Maybe I should just apply. Then I might have a chance to show someone how I could be their storyteller to keep the crowd engaged as they wait in the long lines to go through the venue." I asked Rhonda to take me to the person in charge. I wanted to explain how I saw my role in Dialog in the Dark.

The director had a strong German accent and a stern business manner. I had to move in close to hear her because of all the boisterous people trying to be heard. Apparently I got too close, because she told me to get out of her face and wait in line. I was not only insulted but embarrassed. We were both blind—how else could we communicate in that environment? Dejected, I did as I was told.

With no opportunity to pitch my idea, I threw myself into a pool of legally blind people of all ages and abilities and applied to be a tour guide. I was accepted. We would have two weeks of training, after which they would announce who would be hired as guides. I felt like an American Idol contestant going to Hollywood.

On our way home I said to Rhonda, "I will go ahead and take the two-week training. Hopefully I'll be noticed and become their spokesperson."

From the beginning I doubted my mobility skills for the job and my stamina for all that walking. At sixty-four years old I would be competing with many thirty-year-olds. Many of the applicants were experts at mobility and well-suited for the job as a guide. Dialog in the Dark was a commercial enterprise here in the U.S. The personnel office had chosen mostly visually impaired individuals instead of blind individuals—not that it made much difference. Dark is dark for every-body, but when partially sighted folks stepped into the lighted halls they could maneuver faster.

Two other problems needed to be solved: how to get there and what to do with my guide dog. The exhibition did not allow us to use our dogs for mobility. The dogs would be kept in crates all day while we worked. I knew that my dog, Greta, would not like that. I decided Greta would have to stay home, and I would have to "go it alone."

As I planned how to get to work, I had a huge knot in my stom-ach. The para-transit bus could take two hours, so it wasn't practical. Taking the MARTA transit was the only answer.

I turned to another friend, Betty, whose greatest joy is helping others do what they normally would not or could not do. She and her husband were my karate instructors. They worked diligently in karate class to understand my perspective.

Betty listened intently to my dilemma. She came back with, "Okay, Fiona, I've got it. Here's what we're going to do. I will ride with you on the MARTA train each day to see that you get there safely. I'll go on to work from there. All you have to do is find rides home."

I put out an all-points bulletin to my friends. Several agreed to take turns picking me up after training each day. Excited that everything was falling into place, only one question remained: Could

I master taking the train alone after that? I would think about it another day.

I decided to embark on this new adventure. I arranged for a mobility instructor to help Betty and me navigate my route: the steps, the escalator, the bus stop, and the train station. I had to figure out where to buy tickets, how to put my ticket in the slot, and how to walk through the turnstile.

I had started the Dialog in the Dark venture with enthusiasm, but like much of what I'd done in the past, when it came down to the wire, I was scared to death. The night before my first day of training, I barely slept. Restless, I couldn't stop thinking about how embarrassed I felt to tell Betty my feelings.

The next morning, aboard the MARTA train, I felt like a child about to be left at school for the first time. I leaned into Betty and said, "I cannot do this. I know I jumped at the chance to be here, but there's too much to learn for this senior citizen."

"Come on, we can do it," she said, egging me on.

We did it. We took the train each morning to Atlantic Station and then transferred from train to bus to get to Dialog in the Dark.

But my mind continued to race with doubt. *Why am I doing this? I am nearly sixty-five. I don't have to work. I don't have to do this kind of job. I can make more money telling stories.* I wondered if six hours on my feet—guiding folks through the dark, cajoling them—could really be fun. *Have I gone nuts?*

After three days, Betty admitted, "I just don't feel comfortable with you traveling alone on the train. Sometimes there are scary-looking people around. I will just stay with you each day."

I couldn't let Betty do that. If I was to be working, I had to learn to be independent. But was this the time and place to be seeking independence? I remembered Betty pointed out the first day that some scaffolding and construction work was going on around the building. I couldn't imagine navigating it alone. I did not feel self-sufficient in my mobility training. Taking this leap would force my mobility to improve, if I didn't fall down a shaft first. I wanted to be one of those people who didn't mind asking for directions.

Here I was lying in my bed thinking what an awesome responsibility it was to guide a group of people through the darkness. Some would be silly, scared, awkward, or just curious, but they all would have to trust me, and I would have to be competent.

On the eighth day we had a fire drill that threw me into a panic. I was responsible for getting people safely out of a supposedly burning building. I wondered if I could rise to the occasion in the case of a real fire.

Each night I nursed sore feet and wrote to my friends about my experiences and how excited I was to be a part of this. I had made new friends and enjoyed the camaraderie with my team members. I appeared confident and optimistic about my new endeavor, but inside I struggled. I felt blinder than I had felt in years. Depressed, I prayed. *Dear God, maybe I cannot really do this. Please show me the way.*

The last day I listened to the German founder who was flown in for a press conference. Someone standing in the crowd whispered to me, "Your trainer wants to have a word with you." Betty took me off to the side where he was waiting.

"I wonder why he wants to meet with me?"

He started our meeting with, "How do you think your training is going so far?"

I said, "Fine."

"I understand you bumped your head crossing the street during the tour."

I puffed up with a retort. "The guy behind me told me we were not to use our canes on this first run-through. I put my cane away right before I encountered the lamp post."

My trainer, who was blind himself, continued, "I noticed when your teammates were noisy you ignored them."

"Yes, I thought they were acting like a bunch of obnoxious eighth graders."

"Maybe you didn't hear them."

"Yes, I heard them. I thought it was better to ignore them."

My chest tightened. Was he trying to let me down easy? I'd heard that two people would be cut today. Was I one of them?

A flood of emotion rushed over me. I could hear myself stammering. My trainer gently explained, "I told the guys to be rowdy to see how you would handle it. I am thinking your soft voice and difficulty with hearing would make this job hard for you." I didn't know I was being tested!

I knew what he was getting at. He wanted me to quit. I had never quit anything in my life. I truly do not know what I said after that. I was so embarrassed to admit maybe my hearing wasn't "good enough" or that I didn't fit in. "Betty," I called out. She must have known what was going on because she grabbed me and pulled me away from the situation as the tears spilled from my eyes.

"Betty, get me out of here!" I gasped. "Thank God many of the people here are blind and can't see how I feel."

I didn't want to admit that background noises were a problem. Failure was hard to take. It was enough to be blind. The thought of being too old reverberated in my mind.

Regaining my composure, I turned to Betty. "He wanted me to quit. I did." I shrugged.

As I think back on this, I know my first husband would have been amused at my reaction. He always said I had a little of Scarlett O'Hara in me. When this famous character from *Gone with the Wind* was feeling overwhelmed she would say, "I can't think about that right now. If I do, I'll go crazy. I'll think about that tomorrow." Leaving on Betty's arm, I tried to be optimistic. "Betty, there must be something else for me around the corner."

• • •

Dialog in the Dark is a very important venue for Atlanta. I enjoy bringing my friends and family there for the experience. When the lights dim and the hush falls over the band of six or eight nervous sighted visitors, I feel a little smug because I am the only capable blind one among them. I am not their guide, but I know I will be privy to their reaction in the end because they are my friends. The first time I went back, Marcia and I took my three grandsons. When we stepped out into the daylight, I said, "Boys, do you realize that is what it is like for me all the time?" We chatted about it on the way home and they began to understand.

Ethan piped up with, "I want to bring my friends!" The two older boys, James and Camden, said very little. I think they were trying to process the idea. They had been my sighted guides since they were three and four years old.

Jerry said it best, "It's one thing to close your eyes and walk through a place you have seen; it's quite a new perspective to walk in complete and utter darkness where you have never walked before."

24

The Eyes Have It

The deepest disconnection I have ever felt was with the two people I love the most.

I haven't understood it. I've tried to ignore it. I've even made excuses for it. Have you done this? I am a fix-it personality. When you can't fix it, you can't analyze it either. Sometimes you just have to leave it alone or get away from it—whatever "it" is.

My boyfriend Jerry, who as I've told you became my second husband after I lost my eyesight, often seemed elusive over the course of our many years together. I couldn't grasp why. I decided he didn't love me—he just thought he did. I justified leaving him by thinking he would find out I was right—he would be better off without me. It didn't work.

Two people can love each other and not be compatible as partners. We tried over and over. We couldn't seem to make each other happy.

After years of trying, Jerry gave me new insight—he thought I showed no emotion in my eyes. I was empty, he said. A lot was said.

I know I am not empty. I may be guarded with my emotions, but I could not believe I was without emotion.

The night ended with me feeling more disconnected from him. How could I argue about something which I didn't understand?

Five days later, I had the opportunity to have a serious discussion with my son. The timing was significant.

I asked Chance if he thought my eyes showed no emotion. Did he feel the same way as Jerry? To my surprise, he said he understood what Jerry was saying.

"Mom, I am going to be frank, because I know you can handle it."

I was quite surprised because this was turning into the most personal conversation I'd had with my son in twenty-three years—in fact, dating back to the night I became blind.

Before this talk with Chance, I often felt like I was talking to a wall. I had been so bothered by the lack of communication that I often wound up feeling depressed when I interacted with him. In the past, I had racked my brain trying to determine if this disconnect was because I had done something to hurt him when he was a child. Or did he blame me for the divorce from his father, my first husband? Or now that he was a husband and a father, had he just made up his mind that he didn't like me?

What I was hearing from Chance on this occasion was different. It connected well with the train of thought and discussion that Jerry and I had been through which was a great part of what led to our divorce. So I needed to hear what Chance was saying, not only because I knew my son had insight but because I respected him as a man, even if occasionally he frustrated me, even causing me to doubt his love for me.

"Mom, you show no emotion with your eyes. I can't look at you because it bothers me. So, I just make sure I don't look at you when we talk."

Now I know why he always seems so distracted! It isn't about me—it's about how he can't bear to think about the fact that I can't see.

I asked my best friend if she agreed with these two men—my forty-three-year-old son Chance, who was one year away from being the age I was when I became blind, or my second husband, who was devastated when I became blind, but had to hide it from me.

Marie said, "No, you *do* show feeling in your eyes. I have seen joy, pain, and stress. Perhaps, it's because these two men were the two who were closest to you when it happened. Fiona, you don't realize how hard it has been for the people who love you. We sometimes had to leave the room to keep from crying in front of you."

Men are concrete thinkers. I think they have more difficulty dealing with the experience of trauma and then talking about it. Also, they are fixers. They want to make things right. And, if they can't, they often turn away. I can relate. As I mentioned, I'm a lot like that myself.

Most of us women, on the other hand, love to share and to vent. We analyze everything, even if the result is not a solution. Men need solutions. They need results.

My revelation? Chance does not blame me for anything. He hurts for me. If he could come around more and interact with me more often, he might see me differently—his perspective might change. Maybe we could reconnect.

The eyes have it. What I mean is this: How we "see" our circumstances determines how we act or react. Do we view them as opportunities? Do we see them as challenges? Or does our limited vision—and by this I mean our internal vision located in our heart—cause us to view them as simply devastating events or disasters or situations that can't be overcome, no matter how hard we try, no matter how much God intervenes?

Remember Dialog in the Dark from the previous chapter? One reason I was very eager to be involved with this program was because I knew it would help sighted loved ones of blind people literally see their world. It would also help the general public to do the same.

This would not be so that we blind people could be pitied. Far from it. It would be so that sighted people could learn to experience the *true vision* that blind people eventually develop. That true vision is our coping mechanism. And it is a beautiful thing.

Empty eyes, like Jerry said? I don't think so. My optic nerve may have died but nothing else inside me died. In fact, I came alive in new ways . . . important ways.

For example, I have more resolve, more backbone, more of what some people might call the guts to stand up for what I believe. I am clearer about my principles and no longer afraid to speak up about my limitations and my expectations. I no longer feel responsibility for other people's behavior or reactions. I can only change me, not the other person.

Do you remember my experience with Boy Toy in an earlier chapter? The woman who went with him to the Polaris restaurant and then home to his backyard RV no longer lives in this body and soul called Fiona Page. At that time I was a product of the confusing '50s and '60s when young women of dating age were afraid to bruise men's egos, and young men knew how to manipulate an environment that was ripe with double standards. I'm not saying that only men or only women of those years were to blame. It was our culture.

But, in my life, it led to some distasteful, awkward encounters like the one I described. The truth is I was mad at myself—even more than at Boy Toy—for having to deal with that confrontation. I knew

I hadn't been strong during the moments in that night when I should have been. Of course, by then I was divorced, an acknowledgment that I was vulnerable. I was supposedly a sophisticated woman, but I didn't even know what that meant. Somehow I thought it meant deviating from the polite, people-pleasing person that I was brought up to be. But I didn't know how to pull it off.

Today, I'm no longer vulnerable. I'm not as strong as I hope to become one day, but I am stronger and less vulnerable than I was even when I was sighted. It's true. And it's because "the eyes have it." I have simply decided to view the world and my circumstances with my new true vision.

I promised a surprise ending to the Jerry and Fiona story. Actually, it may not be an ending, but it is certainly a new—and surprising— chapter. It's that new endeavor I mentioned at the end of Dialog in the Dark.

On the twentieth anniversary of my loss of sight, Jerry called. It was a nice conversation. We had not talked in months, although— in the nine years we'd been divorced—we often checked up on one another. And, truth be told, I think we continued to care.

I was touched by his gesture, so I called back and asked to take him out for his birthday. We went with a mutual girlfriend of mine and Jerry's. After the lunch was over and Jerry had left, Jane turned to me and said, "You both still love each other."

I trusted Jane's instinct. That gave me permission to start up again with Jerry. So when the phone calls came, and they began coming every day, I felt good about the reconnection. In a few months, we were seeing each other again but were tenuous about it.

We understand that both of us want to be the parent in the relation- ship, the one who is right. Yet we know that parent-child relationships are unhealthy for couples, and we work hard at overcoming this tendency.

It is hard to see where this new second-chance relationship will go. It's exciting and scary, all at once. It's also quite comfortable.

Jerry and I work every day on improving what began so many years ago when a sighted, divorced woman and a newly separated man made eyes at each other on a dance floor. Our hope is that we will find a way to grow old together.

25

Elephant in the Room

Over the past two decades, I've found myself in situations where I felt I was being treated differently because of my blindness. I know it can be uncomfortable for some people when a blind person suddenly appears in their midst. It isn't their fault. For various reasons, people are often ill at ease in the company of a blind person. They just don't know what to do.

I have dealt with this social uneasiness in numerous ways—usually choosing to make light of it with humor. I rarely admit to anyone that being blind bothers me. No one would make such a conjecture because I usually appear so confident. However, dear reader, there have been times when it was tough to cope. Sometimes insecurity gets the best of me, reminding me of my vulnerability.

This situation slapped me in the face at a party Jerry and I attended with our friends, Jim and Annette. Jim was the only one who knew the hosts—they both worked for the FDIC. Everyone had gathered at

Charles' condo on the lake for a low-country boil before heading to a music concert nearby.

Upon our arrival, we were greeted with a warm welcome by some friendly couples. Jerry immediately found a seat for me on an ultra suede sofa and saw to it that I was seated comfortably. I knew I was placed there because it was the easiest thing to do. Jerry could mingle freely, without me hanging on his arm.

I felt like a fish out of water sitting there, waiting for someone to speak to me. The Swinging Medallions from the '60s were belting out "Double Shot of My Baby's Love" on the boom box across from the sofa.

The first one to spot me was Jackson, the hosts' pet Lab. He greeted me with his toy. We played a quick game of tug-of-war. I was grateful for this interaction. Jackson reminded me of my own yellow Lab, Greta, who had died six months before. We played for a few minutes and then he was off to find another pal.

Next, a couple came over to the sofa, introducing themselves as Mel and Tina. Mel sat next to me. I could tell he was a large, friendly guy. We chatted for a few minutes. I was grateful they were so chatty—it helped put me at ease. When Mel got up to refresh his drink, I turned to Tina and said, "Move closer so I can hear you better. Mel can sit on the other side when he gets back."

Tina moved in and began to share her life story. She told me she was an elementary school guidance counselor. I relaxed even more when I heard this. I, too, had counseling experience back when I was teaching, before becoming blind. Tina was young and refreshing. I knew we had lots to talk about, and I loved to talk.

"We're both educators," I said. Tina listened as I shared my experiences as a teacher and storyteller. While we chatted, I listened for my friends' voices, wondering where they were.

Jerry usually took some time to warm up to strangers. He was so reserved that it often required several beers to loosen him up. *Where was he?* We hadn't been there fifteen minutes when he reappeared, leaned over the sofa, and whispered, "I'm going to the house. I'll be right back."

Just like that, Jerry was gone. He didn't even give me time to respond. Knowing Jerry was just a few steps away if I needed him helped calm my nerves. However, my sense of security left just as suddenly as Jerry.

Weren't they going to eat soon? Who would get my food? Our house was about nine miles away. Many people were in Hiawassee for the Hot Rod Car Show. The parade had started two hours ago. Would Jerry get stuck in traffic? *Why did he leave so abruptly?* That wasn't like him at all. He was my warrior—always Johnny on the spot, taking care of my needs.

I was okay at first, sitting on the sofa chatting with Tina . . . until Tina excused herself. A feeling of quiet desperation hit me. The room felt empty. I couldn't hear any voices. No . . . wait . . . I could hear Annette on the patio. This meant I was alone, except for the blaring boom box. Was everyone moving outside, leaving me inside?

The voices of Jim and Annette filtered into the living room. *I must be sitting near the door to the patio.*

Everyone sounded like they were having a good time out there. I thought about picking up my cane and trying to maneuver myself outside. I had done this many times in the past. Why couldn't I do it now? I didn't know. The unfamiliarity paralyzed me. What if I knock over a lamp? Or trip over Jackson? Several people had brought their little dogs. All I could do was sit and wait.

There are just so many ways you can look like you're having a good time—all by yourself. I tried to place a faint smile on my face. I sensed that wasn't working. I tried to find something interesting to think about. That didn't seem to help either. I just felt foolish and helpless. It was almost comical, attempting facial expressions to hide the panic

I was feeling. Pretending to look like I was deep in thought, I sat there trying hard to fight back the tears.

I know Jerry will come back. This is silly. Put this craziness out of your head, Fiona.

Was he sick? Maybe he forgot something. Okay, maybe he needed ice or more beer.

Why hadn't I grabbed him by the arm? I could have said, "Let me go with you." But he left so fast. I truly felt like the elephant in the room as people passed by from the patio to the kitchen, ignoring me. Everyone was politely stepping around me.

Finally, Jim walked up, bent down, and asked if I needed something. *Yes, I need to break out of this fear,* I thought to myself. "No, thank you, Jim."

I could tell by the clatter of dishes that people were starting to get plates of food. The delicious aroma of shrimp and sausage wafted through the air as people passed through the living room.

Jim stopped once more. "Fiona, are you okay? Do you need anything?"

"No, Jim, I'm fine." By now I wanted to fade into the woodwork.

I wasn't fine. I wanted to bawl. *How silly! Don't be such a baby.* But I couldn't convince myself.

I knew it would be at least thirty minutes before Jerry returned. *How long can I sit here and pretend I'm having fun?* It felt like I was alone for an eternity. Why can't I get off this sofa and be myself?

I knew these feelings were normal, but it was painful, nonetheless. I struggle even now to share this memory. I am a self-assured person who can fearlessly handle most anything. Yet, a simple social event after years of being blind made me crumble inside.

To make matters worse, Charlie came over to offer dinner. "Would you like some shrimp? How can we do this?" He stumbled through the words—clearly feeling awkward.

He was sincerely trying to accommodate me but didn't know how. Any other time I would have been able to rise to the occasion, smiling with southern charm, taking my host's arm to show him the sighted guide technique. I usually could make my guide laugh by saying, "Just think of me as a little shopping bag, hanging on your arm."

Why can't I break into my usual banter? It's my turn to connect. What's wrong with me? Was it because I was sitting, and Charlie was bent over me? It felt so awkward. I sat there, frozen. All I could manage to do was thank him and decline the offer.

Twice now Jim had asked if I wanted to eat. I finally said, "No, I'll just wait for Jerry."

This time he seemed concerned. "Why did Jerry leave? All he said was 'Be right back. Don't worry. It's not good, and it's not bad.'"

Did other people think Jerry acted strangely? "It's not good, and it's not bad" . . . what did that mean? How odd! I wished Jim and Charles would quit fretting over me. If they prodded me too much, I knew I'd lose control. Gathering my courage, I smiled at Jim and waved him on.

Poor Jim came by five times. Finally, I jumped up. "Okay, Jim if it makes you feel better, I'll eat!" What a curt response to his kindness. *What's wrong with me?* Why did such a scene throw me back to my early days of blindness? Would it always be this way?

As soon as I accepted a plate of food, Jerry arrived. Turned out he had ripped his pants and gone home to get a new pair.

The evening ended on a good note. Everyone piled into their cars and boats and headed for the concert. I made up for my earlier behavior by jumping up and dancing to "California Girl." I danced holding onto Jerry's hand as he sat in the front row of the concert. Too shy to dance himself, I knew he was smiling. After breaking the ice, I danced in front of the stage to most of the numbers. Some of the other women in my group were dancing, too.

They like me!

When everyone said their goodbyes, nobody ignored me. They came up to shake my hand or give me a hug, sharing with me just how much they admired my courage. Tina, who had left the sofa abruptly, proudly revealed, "I was the one dancing with you."

"Yes, I know—you are a good dancer."

26

I Can See Clearly Now

Well, my dear reader friend, our journey is nearly over. You have laughed at my life's foibles, peeked at my mistakes, and cringed at my embarrassing moments.

This book may be considered an exercise in self-examination. Perhaps, you see your own reflection in some of these stories. We are a fragile lot, trying to make sense of this life. Sometimes we take a wrong path and have to redirect or reconnect. I can see clearly now that I have learned by paying attention to other perspectives.

In case you are as curious as some, I thought I would throw in the questions I am often asked. I don't mind. People have a need to know.

"Are you angry? Afraid?"

I have been both at times.

"Do you dream in color?"

Yes! I can also see in my dreams. Sometimes I wonder if others in my dreams know I am blind.

"Do you sleep with your eyes opened or closed?"

I have no idea, Silly, I'm asleep!

"Has anyone ever made you feel bad about being blind, or made fun of you?"

Yes, probably more than I know.

"Has anyone ever tried to cheat you?"

Yes. Remind me to tell you the taxi story.

On a Tuesday before Christmas in 1999 I got the verdict at the voice center—absolutely no talking for at least two months, not even a whisper. If I wanted to continue speaking professionally, I had to save my voice.

The next day my friend, Judy, surprised me with warm wishes and a gift. Her visit lifted my spirits. After she left I sat on the floor in the living room to wrap a few last-minute presents. The clock on the mantle that had not worked in years startled me by suddenly chiming. At that very moment I was thinking about my father who had been dead for nine years. Was he trying to console me? He and I were the talkers in the family. No one else could understand how devastating it would be for me to be silent for two months.

I left for Blackshear to be with my family that afternoon. How was I going to communicate without talking? My mother couldn't hear well, and I couldn't see. I remembered the warning about not even whispering. I tried writing notes, but people couldn't read my writing. I spent the holidays sitting at the kitchen table like a Chatty Cathy doll whose batteries had run out.

I returned home, glad to be away from the pressure to talk.

A few months earlier I had rented my basement apartment to Marcia, a friend of my mentor, Clyde. She had edited his book. Remember how he spotted me on the airplane and asked the passenger next to me to read aloud *Cancer, the Gift of Life*? He had orchestrated our meeting—since Marcia and I both shared an interest in writing, he thought we needed to get acquainted.

I wrote Marcia a note about the doctor's orders.

Marcia responded with, "Fiona, maybe this is the time to start writing your memoir."

I scoffed at the idea. Me? A writer? So many people told me over the years that I should write a book, but I never thought too much about it.

"It will keep you entertained," she said. "I can come up each night and proofread your work."

That night as I lay in bed I thought about what Marcia said. A few days later, feeling better, I sat down to my talking computer and started writing. I had stored up so many stories from the twelve years I had been blind. Could I remember them all? Why hadn't I kept a journal? My fingers flew across the keyboard like they were doing the talking. I poured out my heart and soul every night. The anxiety swelled in my chest as I waited to read Marcia's emailed comments. To hear JAWS, the screen reading software, speak her words would reveal the answer I sought—did I have any writing talent? Only time would tell if I had the courage to publish my words.

Here we are nearing the end of this journey. You, my new friend, have the option—if you are curious—to read the second part of this book where I share tales of my childhood and those of my family's heritage. The strongest roots of my existence are my heroes: Mama and Grandma Morgan. Everybody needs heroes.

You have seen how my life shattered in a short six hours. I have learned much in this time as well as been reminded of the things I already knew. Feeling invincible can make you vulnerable and careless. Never burn your bridges. Be careful who you choose as mentors.

Persevere. Remember 2 Corinthians 5:7: " . . . *live by faith, not by sight.*" Determination runs deeper than you think.

What keeps spouting from my mouth each time I speak to an audience is, "We all want to fit in, to belong." Making connections with others and keeping those relationships gives us power in the darkest moments. Throughout this book, you have heard me mention the strength and courage of my mother. Her favorite words were, "Every cloud has a silver lining. Be patient, Fiona."

On that momentous night in September I died on the life-flight trip, but God granted me another chance. I believe it was to grow spiritually and help others to see clearly their own true vision.

Top: Graham's Grocery and Gas Station (1940s) was originally built by Kenny Graham's father-in-law, John S. Morgan.

Right: Kenny outside the original Morgan house (1942).

Right: Nana standing outside her house (1942).

Bottom: Fiona and Nana with the new family car (1946).

Fiona soon after she was married to Bill (1965).

Jerry and Fiona about the time they were married (1993).

Introduction to Root Causes

This section is important because so many have asked—where do you get your motivation, your drive, your optimism?

My mother's spirited courage and no nonsense attitude about her disability fit me like a glove. The color she painted in her stories falls from my mouth without effort. Storytelling just comes naturally.

I wear the same cloak of fearlessness as my maternal grandmother whom you will meet in "Makin' Eyes." This amazing story tells of two country folk from south of the Mason-Dixon Line who find each other amidst gentile society in Virginia.

A spark of romance weaves its way through my life in the story of my mother and father's courtship. "If I Didn't Care" tells their love story. How I hope our descendants will learn to recapture the innocence of that era of my parents' generation. I don't want to think innocence is gone forever.

When you read "A Dose of Reality" you will understand the fears and thoughts threaded throughout my journey. I have seen the face of prejudice early in my life as the daughter of a handicapped woman and later in my life as a person with a disability. It is shaded differently now than in the '60s. Then it was blatant in South Georgia where I grew up. Now it's subtle and disguised, but present nonetheless.

In "Order Out of Chaos" you will learn about why I am attracted to orderliness. Since as long as I can remember, I have liked things to be orderly. That has come in handy after becoming blind. What if I was sloppy all of the time?

"The Twelfth of Never" and "Mama Got Liberated at the P.W." will give you a sense of the way we Morgan women wear our spunk with a touch of rebellion.

We all are products of our upbringing, perhaps more than we know. Our family heritage is the fabric of who we are. Through these stories you may find some answers to the question of what makes Fiona tick.

1

Makin' Eyes

The story of Grandma Juliette comes from the snatches of stories I heard as a child. My grandmother was born in 1880 and died in 1941, the year before I was born. She descended from the Harrisons of Virginia and was related to two Presidents of the United States—William Henry and Benjamin Harrison.

"We have a photograph of President Benjamin Harrison," Mama said one day while working in our family store.

As a little girl, I was very proud to be related to Presidents of our country. The next day I went to school and bragged about the picture.

"Your great-grandfather, Jacque de Butts, came to this country from France when he was a very young man. He met his wife at the house of Theodore Harrison, a relative of President Harrison. Grandfather dropped the 'de' in his last name as many immigrants did in those days."

Mama didn't know much about her grandparents because they died before my grandma reached adulthood. Most of what Mama knew came from two sources: family stories and her mother's steamer trunk. Mama stored this musty trunk inside a long closet that connected our two bedrooms. When I was little I played for hours in that big closet. I remember reading the letters inscribed above the latch of the old trunk, J-u-l-i-e-t-t-e. Opening the trunk, crawling inside, and playing with the magical things it held was a favorite pastime of mine.

One day I found a long black taffeta dress and a lonely leather high button shoe. I tried on both. She must have had the tiniest feet because the shoe nearly fit my little girl foot! Mama started the tale, "Your grandmother wore these shoes when she was seventeen years old."

"Where did she get all these postcards?" Picking up a stack of cards, I let them cascade down like a waterfall. Photographs of the Taj Mahal and Leaning Tower of Pisa flashed before my eyes.

"Well, your Uncle Paul left home at fifteen, I think it was. He joined the Merchant Marines for the adventure. Those postcards were sent to Mother. He wanted her to 'see the world through his eyes.' Do you remember the cuckoo clock he sent last Christmas? And the wooden shoes from Holland?"

I nodded, remembering the fun we had when those presents arrived at our grocery store. That was one of the reasons I liked meeting the mailman.

"Uncle Paul sent your grandmother a postcard from every seaport he visited."

I enjoyed playing with these cards as much as I enjoyed listening to Mama's stories. Those picture postcards took me to faraway places.

On another trunk adventure I found a round pewter pot about the size of a half dollar with a tiny hinged lid. Placing it in my palm, I pinched the thin lid open. Resting on a bed of red velvet was a string of glass beads. I grabbed them and tried pulling them over my head. They didn't fit!

Mama took them from me. "This is not jewelry, Fiona. These are prayer beads. Your grandmother went to a Catholic school when she was a young girl. Her family was Catholic."

"What's a Catholic?"

She smiled. "It's a religion."

"Are we Catholics?"

"No, we're Methodists." I didn't know the difference, but I didn't ask any more questions.

Juliette, the youngest of three, lived on a small farm in rural eastern Virginia—maybe a day's ride by carriage from the coast. The Morgans had enough food from cultivating the small farm to sustain their family of five, but winters were hard. To support his family, Jacque became a tobacco taster for R.J. Reynolds Tobacco Company. Tobacco tasting was an important job—if the tobacco was bitter, the crop was no good.

Juliette's mother died from a high fever when Juliette was only seven years old (we think she died of scarlet fever.) Juliette took over her mother's responsibilities, caring for the house and three men. It was up to her brothers to work the farm. Life was about survival in the 1880s, especially for small time farmers like the Butts.

By the time Juliette was fourteen, her brothers left home to start their own families. She never saw or heard from them again. Life was infinitely more difficult after her brothers left, but Juliette faithfully maintained the garden and kept the housekeeping up for her father. She gathered eggs, milked the cow, and fed the animals.

Over the next year, Jacque's eyesight gradually worsened until he reached the point that he could no longer drive the wagon to the Reynolds plantation. His extraordinary ability to determine the quality of the tobacco was known by all, including his boss. Unwilling to lose one of his most valuable employees, Mr. Reynolds sent a carriage to transport Jacque to and from work each day.

The fall before Juliette turned fifteen, her father got whooping cough and his condition weakened. Despondent over his inability to take care of his daughter, Jacque spent months in bed. He passed away before Juliette's sixteenth birthday. The frozen winter ground prevented a proper burial, so Juliette had no choice but to wrap her father in blankets and put him in the root cellar until spring.

Juliette knew she could not take care of her home all alone. Neighbors were miles away. Recalling her mother's words, "Be proud. You came from good stock, young lady," Juliette knew what to do. She remembered her mother had a brother in Virginia Beach. Juliette had not been there, but she thought it wasn't far. Mother had told her he was wealthy. *Perhaps he would be kind enough to help me*, she thought.

Juliette decided to write her Uncle Ted and ask for his help. Juliette's mother, an educated woman herself, taught her children to read and write. It was rare for country girls to have such a privilege, but education was very important to the Morgans. Writing the letter was the easy part, getting it delivered in the middle of winter was another matter. She wrote the letter and waited for spring.

At the first sign of warm weather, Juliette heard Peddler Joe whistling around the bend and ran down the path to meet him, smiling broadly. He was kind and friendly. He assured her Virginia Beach was on his route to the sea. He would have the letter delivered within the week! Juliette waited patiently, filling her days with chores. After all, she still had to survive.

Ted was quite surprised to receive the letter. Concerned for his sister's child, whom he had never met, he made plans to leave immediately. He called his only daughter, Jeanne, into his library. "You have a country cousin you will soon meet."

Jeanne made no comment about her father's plans. He was a serious, no nonsense man who commanded the household with an iron fist.

A knock on the door took Juliette by surprise. Peeking out the window, she saw a tall, well-dressed, distinguished gentleman standing at her door. *Could this be my uncle?* Sheepishly she opened the door of her modest farm house.

"I am your mother's brother and you must be Juliette," he said in a firm deep voice. He took her hand, bowing politely. Accustomed to taking charge, he said, "We shall leave right away—pack only what you must and I have someone arriving tomorrow to dispose of the farm animals and other details."

Stunned by his forwardness, Juliette did as she was told. She retrieved her mother's valise from the bedroom and packed a few cherished mementos. Thoughts raced through her mind as she packed the two dresses she owned. *Here is this complete stranger standing in my home orchestrating my future.* She was not sure she would like this new life.

Closing the door to the only home she had ever known and stepping into her uncle's fine carriage, Juliette felt a tingle of excitement. As the carriage drove away, she turned, peeked through the carriage curtain, and whispered goodbye to her past.

After a long silence and several miles, Juliette's uncle spoke. "You, my dear, will learn to be a lady," he said as he looked over his spectacles at her simple dress and shabby shoes. "I will provide for your welfare including school. You are already enrolled in a fine Catholic school for girls with my daughter Jeanne." She could never have imagined going to school, let alone the life this carriage was taking her toward.

Once her uncle finished speaking, Juliette murmured a prayer, "I will hold my head high and do as I am told, Mother." The first order of business would be to get to know her cousin Jeanne.

When the carriage made a sharp turn into the long driveway, Juliette knew she was at the entrance to her new home. An iron fence embraced the lovely gardens of the estate. She could see the kitchen attached to the back of the main house by way of a breezeway. The stately Victorian house rested on a tree-lined cobble street with wooden sidewalks, called boardwalks, along both sides. A veranda wrapped halfway around the house was bracketed by two tall, round, pointy roofs on either side.

Uncle Ted introduced Juliette to the three servants he employed—a chamber maid, a gardener, and a cook. He explained she was only to speak to these servants when giving them orders. The gardener's smile warmed Juliette's heart. She could not have known how much she would appreciate his smiles nor could she have known how much his friendliness would come to mean to her.

Next, Uncle Ted introduced her cousin who was just a year older than Juliette. Her father assigned Jeanne the task of helping her country cousin adjust to city life. Something about her demeanor made Juliette suspect cousin Jeanne did not "cotton to" her new assignment. Juliette followed her cousin upstairs to her room. She noticed each room had a fireplace and the hallways had gas lights. Jeanne opened the door and stepped aside for her cousin to see. Juliette gasped. "My, I haven't ever seen a roof on a bed before! It is bea-u-ti-ful!"

Putting her fingers over her lips, Jeanne smothered her laughter. "Father has arranged for our seamstress to come fit you for two new dresses and a velvet cloak. If you measure up Father will give you such a wardrobe as I have!" Juliette had no idea what it meant to "measure up."

Juliette's crude homespun dresses and shabby shoes were immediately thrown away. Until she was fitted for her very own wardrobe, Jeanne let Juliette borrow a couple of her dresses. A few days later two nice dresses of silk and taffeta arrived along with a pair of leather high button shoes. Certainly not the kind of apparel a country girl would wear, but giving up her old wardrobe was a blessing.

That night, gazing at the fancy clothing her uncle provided, Juliette couldn't imagine wanting more. But then thoughts of home and her mother and father made her pause. Knowing she could not allow herself to dwell on the past, she told herself to stop feeling homesick. "Be thankful for what you have," she whispered. Yet sitting in her dark room, Juliette longed for her brothers to find her.

• • •

On Juliette's first day of school she made her way downstairs, giggling at her squeaky high button shoes. The giggles stopped a few steps later when she realized the leather squeezed her ankles and hurt her tiny feet. Next she noticed that her taffeta dress rustled every time she took a step. "I can hardly breathe, all bound up like a rabbit caught in a trap!" Her sleeves bound her arms all the way down to her ruffled wrist. Her neck was adorned with stiff lace.

Just as Juliette gagged, Jeanne began to laugh. "Juliette, the lace at your neck is from Spain," she explained with snobbish authority.

So many changes! Juliette loved her new dresses, but she still wasn't sure if she was going to like this new life. *I think I want to go to school. But I don't want to be a lady if I have to be a snob like Jeanne! I like her all right, but I want to be myself!*

Jeanne taught Juliette how to wrap her long, black hair around her fingers to form curls on top of her head. Pinning a small gray veiled hat over her curls, Jeanne said, "A lady must always shield her eyes in public," said Jeanne.

She handed Juliette a pair of black gloves.

"Why do I have to wear gloves? It's not cold!"

Jeanne ignored the question. Trying to teach Juliette how to be a lady gave her a sense of superiority. She doubted that anyone could turn this rough lump of coal into a fine diamond.

Juliette was determined to make her cousin like her, but turning into a lady was another matter! For now, Juliette didn't mind being bossed around by her cousin. She admired Jeanne's straightforward manner. At least she knew where she stood.

The two cousins finally left the house, walked to the end of the street, and boarded a horse-drawn streetcar. Traveling to catechism classes, they sat in the next to the last bench. The girls made this trip five days a week for two months. During this time, Juliette finally began to feel like she was getting to know her cousin. Sitting in the back of the streetcar, they whispered to themselves and giggled about the other passengers. Having a little fun together seemed to cement their relationship.

One day a handsome young man took notice of the girls. Something about the attractive dark-haired young girl intrigued him. He could tell by her comments that she was not an aristocrat, but then neither was he.

In business circles he was referred to as J.S. Morgan, but his friends called him John. He was twenty-nine years old. He had traveled to Virginia Beach from North Carolina to seek his fortune. Although he owned a successful liquor store, he knew few people in Virginia Beach. His goal was to become rich but he didn't delude himself into thinking he would ever be included in Virginia society.

One crisp October morning, Juliette met John Seth Morgan's gaze as he climbed onto the streetcar. She leaned toward Jeanne and asked, "What do you think of that gentleman over there?"

"He is handsome and probably rich. Hmmm, he does look like quite the successful businessman," Jeanne said, looking him over.

"How can you tell that?" Juliette asked.

"Look at that suit! It's made of fine camel's hair wool. Probably imported and tailored just for him. He is not crippled so the walking stick is a fashion statement. The quality of the stick indicates his station in life. Look at the gold-carved handle," Jeanne said. "Yes, I think he is definitely rich."

Juliette agreed that he did look dignified with spats over his shoes for protection. Only wealthy men cared about mud splattering from the horse-drawn buggies and carriages.

Juliette secretly looked forward to seeing J.S. Morgan on her daily streetcar rides. She loved "making eyes" with him, a characteristic she would pass along to future generations. Certain that the veil on her hat allowed her to examine his face without him knowing, she would gaze at him unabashedly. His camel colored bolo had a narrow brim, allowing her to see directly into his vivid blue eyes. But one morning, she was forced to look away quickly when she saw the amused look on his face. He had caught her at her little game. If Jeanne had noticed, she didn't say.

J.S. Morgan watched Juliette for a couple of weeks, contemplating what he needed to do to meet her. The societal norms of the time did not allow a stranger to introduce himself to a woman. Only a formal introduction arranged by someone in the ladies' social circle was acceptable. Clearly these two did not travel in the same circles, so it was unlikely they would ever meet in an appropriate manner. He knew he had to create a way to initiate an introduction.

J.S. soon came up with a clever plan and put it into action one afternoon. He boarded the streetcar and sat on the back row behind the girls' favorite seat. When Juliette saw J.S. seated directly behind her regular seat, she glanced up, fluttering her eyelashes. She gave him a demure smile before sitting next to her cousin. He tipped his hat, as he did every day, and waited patiently for the girls to begin their schoolgirl chatter. Certain they were adequately distracted from his presence, he began using the tip of his cane to carefully snag a loose strand of Juliette's hair from under her hat. J.S. proceeded to meticulously attach the long strand to the streetcar cable used to signal her stop. As Jeanne reached for the cable, she caught a glimpse of the gentleman behind her. His smile confirmed her suspicions and she was onto his secret. When Juliette stood up she felt a tug. Next thing she knew her hat fell off. Startled, she fell backwards. Waiting with open arms, J.S. caught her, gallantly retrieved her hat, and introduced himself.

Jeanne jerked Juliette away before she had time to tell him her name. Undaunted, J.S. Morgan followed the girls off the streetcar, keeping a respectable distance. Juliette let Jeanne open the gate outside the estate while she stole a glance to see if the handsome young man was nearby. He grinned when she met his gaze. Giggling, Juliette rushed in the door behind Jeanne and ran to the front window.

"What are you doing? Father will be furious!"

Juliette didn't care. Looking outside, she saw the gentleman motion the old gardener over to the gate. The two spoke and exchanged something. *What did he hand to the old gardener?* Juliette brushed past her cousin, avoiding her curious stare, and rushed upstairs. She shut her door, breathless and excited. Her heart was thumping wildly. *Could he? Would he? Did he write something to her?*

Later that evening the gardener knocked on her door with the nightly firewood delivery. She opened her door and immediately noticed a twinkle in his eyes. "Mr. Morgan paid me fifty cents to deliver this note, Miss Juliette." She thought her heart would jump out of her bosom! Never before had she been so thankful that her mother taught her to read and write.

For the next two months the old man conspired, delivering daily passionate letters between J.S. and Juliette. It didn't hurt that he was paid well. Every night at midnight Juliette locked her bedroom door to read the precious letters from her beloved J.S. Juliette kept up this charade because she could not afford to trust Jeanne with her secret.

John Seth Morgan proposed eloquently in his letters to his sweet Juliette and she replied with a profound yes! They had never touched, kissed, or even uttered each other's names but they could not wait to be together. Knowing her uncle would never allow them a proper courtship, they decided to elope.

In his thirty-first letter John outlined their runaway plans. Late one November night Juliette packed her valise with a few of her mother's things. The only outfit she took was what she had on—the taffeta and lace black one and leather high button shoes. Opening the window, she leaned out and began trilling like a small bird to signal her lover. When she heard his responding low whistle, Juliette climbed out the window and landed on the roof below. She quietly slid her valise over the edge where John was waiting. Crawling on her stomach, she inched across the tin roof toward the drainpipe. Swinging the rustling skirts over the pipe, the lovers touched for the first time. "John Seth," she whispered as he swept her into his waiting arms. A driver and black carriage were waiting at the street corner to whisk them away. John arranged for a friend of his to marry them. The judge's house was only a block away.

He also rented a small house not far from his liquor store. That night they settled into their tiny love nest, happy as two lovebirds.

Juliette's first order of business was to contact her uncle. He had been so kind to take her in after her father died. She did not want to be ungrateful. She only wanted to be with her husband. After spending several hours trying to pen the letter, she finally settled on a brief note. The damage was done. If he was angry, there was nothing she could do. "Dear Uncle Ted, I cannot find the words to express my gratitude for your kindness and generosity. Please understand and know that I am safe and happily married to Mr. John Seth Morgan."

Unfortunately, Ted heard about the elopement before receiving the letter. He was furious! John's property manager informed him that Ted Harrison owned the warehouse he rented for his business and was not pleased to know Juliette's husband was selling liquor out of it. How long would it be before he asked John to move?

When news of this fury reached the Morgans, John told Juliette it would be best for them to move. "Your uncle could make trouble for us. He is a very influential man."

Juliette wondered, *What kind of trouble could her Uncle Ted make for them?*

That Saturday John closed shop at nine in the evening and walked home. They didn't live far—four blocks. The night was clear and cold with a bright full moon. Two men dressed in dark clothing surprised John from behind. They hit him over the head with a blunt object and he fell into a heap under a willow tree.

"He's dead!" groaned one of the thugs. "Let's get out of here before someone comes!" Grabbing what they could from the body, they fled.

Luckily, John's Saturday night helper had locked up the warehouse shortly after John left and was headed home along the same path. Snow was a huge black man with snow white hair and a gimp leg from the war. A black man might have been afraid to stop when he saw a white man lying on the ground, but Snow thought he recognized the clothes. "Mr. John, is that you? Is you all right?" Snow bent down to see if he was breathing. His boss was unconscious, lying on the ground under the willow tree in a pool of his own blood. Snow quickly hoisted him onto his back and carried him home.

As John recovered, Juliette expressed how frightened she was by the incident. She had so many questions. Was it possible John just happened to be in the wrong place at the wrong time—a coincidence? Did her uncle arrange this and, if he did, how could he do such a horrible thing? It was unthinkable.

John was right—they needed to move away from Virginia Beach. It didn't take long for him to convince Juliette that Atlanta, Georgia was a new city, full of opportunity. Once again they left, under the cover of darkness. This time they would travel a long time. After many detours and a year on the road, John fulfilled his promise. That's another story for another time.

2

If I Didn't Care

Our mother was a successful business woman most of her life. In fact, she ran her own tax preparation business until she was eighty years old. But her number one priority was taking care of Daddy and her two daughters. Daddy was the wind beneath Mama's wings. He saw in her very special qualities: strength, determination, and conviction. I believe he was blind to her disability. My sister and I know we had very special parents. They loved each other for fifty years. Daddy died the November after that fiftieth wedding anniversary. Mama died sixteen years after Daddy.

In October 2009, our family home was demolished in Blackshear, Georgia. Daddy built that house in 1962 on the same property where my grandparents' house once stood. My sister called to tell me they found Mama's love letters to Daddy in the walls of our childhood home. I guess he put them behind the walls for safekeeping. This is their love story.

• • •

In 1939, Kenny Graham sputtered into Waycross with five bucks in his pocket and one last gift box of sculptured rose-scented soap in his trunk. The Depression had pushed many young men to join public work relief programs established by President Franklin D. Roosevelt. With no jobs available, Kenny joined the Civilian Conservation Core for a while. He sent most of his earnings home to help support his three younger sisters. This didn't last long, though. He decided to seek his fortune by jumping the rails and joining the hobos. Kenny landed in southern Texas where he met up with two Jewish fellows. Impressed by how they could sell anything, Kenny persuaded them to teach him their spiel. After that, he became a traveling salesman.

As soon as he made enough money, Kenny bought an old jalopy. He discovered he was good at door to door sales. He called on the farmers' wives around Texas and Missouri, offering them a free box of decorative rose soap just for trying out Proctor and Gamble's new Oxydol washing powders. Never mind that most of the farm women didn't have new-fangled washing machines to use the soap powder. They were delighted to get a free gift just for trying it out. Folks welcomed strangers because they didn't have much company living on large country farms. They didn't have a reason to be suspicious or afraid. Kenny was a nice looking fellow. He had a Cary Grant look about him with his dark hair swept over fashionably. His heavy brows hooded twinkly, deep set brown eyes and a charming grin, which disarmed many a lady. Working his way east, Kenny sold soap door to door from Texas to Georgia.

When he arrived in Waycross, he noticed a big sign advertising Miss Irene's boarding house, "Home of Good Southern Cooking." Kenny decided this would be a good place to rent a room and have a Sunday dinner.

Stepping inside, Kenny flipped his grey fedora onto the hat rack. He glanced around at the crowded long tables, looking for an open seat. Trying to decide where to sit, his eyes fell on two attractive young ladies. Kenny sat down next to the redhead, the prettier one. If you have ever heard of the boarding house reach, it means having long enough arms to reach the large bowls of delicious fried chicken and mashed potatoes. You more than likely would sit next to a stranger or a neighbor. It was like eating at a school lunchroom with all the food already on the table—only this was home-cooked goodness!

Reaching for a biscuit, he tried to introduce himself. They glanced up for a second before resuming their conversation. He was never at a loss for words, but the two young ladies politely passed the bowls while continuing their gossip.

While eavesdropping on their conversation, Kenny gathered that the girl sitting next to him was named Nanette and the other was her sister, Berta. They were talking about Nannette's best friend, Nana. The conversation went like this:

"Imagine being featured in a syndicated newspaper column like 'Ripley's Believe It Or Not!'" Nanette said.

"Our girlfriend might become famous!" Berta replied.

"Nana says that Greyhound wants top billing, whatever that means," Nannette continued.

"Well, she *is* their employee, you know. I guess they are entitled to tell her what they want. Having your legs amputated is no easy way to get publicity. Are you sure Nana will do this?"

Nannette hesitated. This pause gave Kenny an opportunity to jump in, "Pardon me, ladies, I'm curious. Don't mean to be rude, but what happened to your friend's legs?"

Nannette passed the biscuits again, ignoring his question. Kenny got the message, so he ate quietly and tried to listen for more details about Nana. He didn't listen closely, though, and missed the part about Nana getting two wooden legs at the age of fourteen.

Ripley's indeed wanted Miss Nana featured in their museum. They recently interviewed her for the "Ripley's Believe It or Not" newspaper column. No female had been known to have such a birth defect. Her legs were severely crippled: One was missing a small bone and both feet curved inward. They were impossible to stand on, so she crawled most of her life. When she was thirteen years old, she asked her mother to find someone to remove her useless legs. Her mother searched until she found Dr. Michael Hoke at Piedmont Hospital in Atlanta. Dr. Hoke was well-known for a new development called prostheses. Nana was told she was the first woman to walk on two wooden legs and Ripley's wanted to share her story.

Although Kenny read the popular syndicated newspaper column, he had never heard of Nana. Was she so odd that Ripley's would make a wax figure of her for their museum?

Not making much headway with his flirting, Kenny decided to take a walk. His old car was on its last legs, which might cause him to be in Waycross until he figured out a plan. It appeared that this Yankee was stuck in the Deep South. What else could he do?

Remembering that Berta mentioned Nana worked at the Greyhound bus station, Kenny decided to walk there first. He could see it was just a few blocks away. He hoped he might get to meet this incredible gal. *She must have such a difficult life,* he thought.

Until President Franklin D. Roosevelt's time a person with a disability was rarely seen in public. Even he did not allow himself to be filmed in a wheelchair. People with severe distortions were hidden away at home or in sanitariums. Some even joined a carnival freak show.

Kenny found the bus depot crowded with men in uniforms. War had broken out in Europe. Many feared the U.S. would enter the war soon. All service branches were calling in their reserves.

Kenny strode around the busy terminal looking for the crippled girl. He expected she might have a platform on wheels to get around. What kind of work could a handicapped person do, especially one with no legs?

After nosing around, Kenny went to the lunch counter, ordered a cup of coffee, and began watching the people. As he scanned the crowd, his eyes locked with a pair of sparkling green eyes. *Wow! What a looker! She looks about twenty-four years old, like me.* As he stared, she glanced up from behind the ticket counter and flashed him an inviting l smile.

This was his chance! He sauntered over and took his place in line. When his turn came he cleared his throat and asked, "When's the next bus to Peoria, Illinois?"

"The bus you want just left about an hour ago," she replied.

Kenny felt the chemistry sizzle with this cute little brunette even though she was *all business*! He was convinced she would go out with him if he persisted. His original mission to find Nana was forgotten. This young Yankee would get a date with this babe for sure! All he had to do was come up with another city to inquire about and get back in line.

The ticket agent did not have time for this foolishness. After three tries, she was terse with him. "Are you sure you know where you want to go, mister?"

"I want to go to dinner with you, sweetheart," he replied with a big grin.

"Get lost, buddy! I'm busy here and you are holding up the line."

His hopes were not squashed. Kenny started plugging nickels in the jukebox playing his favorite song, "If I Didn't Care" by the Inkspots, grinning every time she looked his way.

He left that afternoon and returned the next day. Once again, Kenny got in line. "How about dinner, doll?" he asked.

She was annoyed, but a little intrigued with his persistence. He obviously was not going away. Warming to his charm, she agreed to meet him after work.

Hmmm, maybe this guy would be fun, she thought.

So Kenny waited at the lunch counter until five o'clock. To kill time, he started pumping the waitress for information about his future date. He didn't even know her name.

The gal behind the counter looked a little like Bugs Bunny. When she told him her name was Bugs Murray, he didn't ask why. No need to. Kenny was in luck—Bugs loved to gossip and she knew his five o'clock date by name.

"I forgot to ask this doll her name. Do you know it?"

"Yep. It's Nana," Bugs replied.

"Not the Nana with no legs?" he blurted. "But she's too tall!"

Bugs laughed, "You've been flirting with her all afternoon, mister! She got her picture in the *Florida Times Union* recently. No joke! Ripley's Believe It or Not wants her to be in their museum because she has two artificial legs. She let a doctor amputate them when she was thirteen. Until she got her wooden legs, she couldn't stand up! When they handed her crutches, she just crossed her arms and said, 'If I have to use crutches you can just have these legs back.'"

"Is that so?" said Kenny.

"You know what? She learned to walk without them crutches!" Bugs beamed proudly, as though she had some stake in it.

"Wow!" Kenny was fascinated. He couldn't wait to get to know this remarkable gal.

At five o'clock, Kenny anxiously waited outside the depot for his date. Leaning against his jalopy, he watched as the door to the office opened. Nana walked out a little stiffly, but Kenny didn't notice. He was smitten. Out of nowhere two huge bus drivers swooped up Nana and put her on the waiting bus. She never had a chance to protest. Kenny was stunned! Who were these men? Why did they put Nana on the bus?

The next day, Kenny returned to the bus depot with a pocket full of nickels. He spent the early part of the day putting money into the jukebox, waiting for Nana to talk to him. His persistence paid off. When they spoke, she answered some of his questions about the previous day. Kenny learned Nana had a boyfriend and that the bus drivers who whisked her onto the bus were her boyfriend's buddies. That was the bus she took each day to her parent's house in Blackshear.

Despite this news of a boyfriend, Kenny didn't give up. He came back every day for a week until he wore her down with his charm. The boyfriend soon became history. For six months, Kenny and Nana were a hot item. Nana introduced him to all her friends, even her buddy, Hoover, who was one of the bus drivers.

For the next few months Nana did what she could to help Kenny find a job. He finally found work in Augusta, about 150 miles north of Blackshear. The young couple tried their best to stay in touch by writing letters to each other. They created their very own delivery system using the bus route to and from Augusta. Nana's bus driver friends diligently delivered every single letter, including the one where Kenny proposed. Immediately after receiving his proposal, Nana quit the bus station and saw to it that Kenny got her job. They planned to marry on March 23, 1940.

Nana bought her peignoir and pill box hat with veil at The Fashion Shoppe. She loved pretty clothes, especially lingerie. Nana made her own navy blue wedding suit in two days. She had sewn most of her own clothes since she was a teenager.

Nana knew it wouldn't be easy telling her parents, especially her father, about her engagement. He had not approved of his crippled daughter accepting the college scholarship to become a legal secretary. Now she wanted to marry this Yankee stranger? But she desperately wanted her father's approval. It was important to her that her parents be there on her wedding day. When it came time to tell her parents, she threw her fox fur scarf around her shoulders, marched into their living room, and asked boldly, "Papa, Mama, I'm getting married this afternoon and I want you to be there with me."

Her father frowned in dismay. "I have always taken care of you. When a family member has an affliction, it is the father's duty to see to it that his loved one is cared for. I do not approve of this marriage. Humph, not to mention he's a Yankee!"

Nana's mother silently stood by her husband. Years ago she had searched for medical help for her daughter. Her husband did not participate in this, but he did not stop her. Now she felt she had to defer to his wishes even though she longed to be at her daughter's wedding.

That fateful day, Kenny and Nana walked out of her childhood home on Highway 82 and hitchhiked the nine miles to the First Baptist

Church in Waycross. Red, a cab driver friend, saw them all dressed up walking down the street and hollered. "Where ya going?"

"To get married."

"Hop in. I'll give you a ride." After driving them the last block to the church, he joined them as their witness.

After the ceremony, the newlyweds met up with some friends to celebrate at the Blackshear Bowl, a local nightspot. At the end of the night, one of their buddies asked, "Where can I drop you off?"

"Home, James!" Nana retorted.

Yes, Nana took her bridegroom to her parents' two bedroom stucco home on Highway 82. The bedrooms were joined by a bathroom and large closet. You could walk all the way through the closet to get from one bedroom to another.

They crept noiselessly into Nana's room, trying not to wake her parents. Kenny undressed in the adjoining closet while her parents, unknowingly, slept. Nana slipped into her lovely white peignoir, propped her artificial legs next to the bed, and transferred herself from the wheelchair she kept in the room to the bed. Kenny stepped out of the closet, humming his favorite song, "If I Didn't Care." Ready for bed, he winked and said, "Sweetheart, I am your loving husband here to take care of you for the rest of our lives."

He wrapped his arms around her. "Now let's take off that cute little hat."

Our family was very open and loved to joke. My sister and I would giggle when Mama teased Daddy about undressing in the closet on their wedding night. Daddy would kid her about the hat. We grew up hearing them tease each other. But it is true. Kenny Graham took care of his bride, Nana, for fifty years right there on Highway Avenue.

My grandfather brought his family—three children and his wife—to Blackshear in 1916 after reading about the almost tropical climate. He purchased the property where he built his house and grocery store. Mama and Daddy took over the business when my grandmother died suddenly. A year later, my grandfather had a stroke. The stern man who declared, "We take care of our own!" found himself being taken care of by his Yankee son-in-law. The fickle finger of fate dealt him this irony.

After almost forty years of service, the grocery store closed in 1955. My parents reopened it in 1957 as a soft ice cream store and it eventually evolved into a family style restaurant. When my brother-in-law joined the family, it became known as Graham-Tsaklis restaurant and Dari Kream. The restaurant was open from 1957 until 1985.

Daddy preceded Mama by sixteen years in reaching those heavenly gates. She left us when she was ninety-four years old. At both their funerals, the men and women who had either been an employee or patron of their businesses stood up to share their memories and respect for our Mama and Daddy. We could not have been prouder.

3
Twelfth of Never

Blackshear, Georgia in 1955 was much like a southern version of *Happy Days*, the popular 1970s TV show. My hometown had a population of only about six thousand. Even so, we called ourselves "city slickers." We lived next door to Morgan Grocery, the store Mama inherited from my grandfather. Our white stucco house with lavender blue trim and the matching grocery store was located on Highway 82, the main street in town. When I was young, I enjoyed sitting on the fence watching cars and trucks whiz by me. After puberty hit, though, I preferred watching boys.

Some of my favorite memories are from when I was a preteen. My life consisted of cheerleading, playing basketball, roller skating, and going to the movies on Saturday and Sunday afternoons. I could walk to the Royal Theater in town, but I was required to drag my little sister along as my chaperone. That was annoying!

My parents were smart cookies. They enclosed the front porch of our house to create a dance floor for me and my seventh grade friends. This was a shrewd move. Being twelve and a truly red-blooded girl, they could see me becoming boy crazy.

My parents' attempt to keep my social life under watchful eyes was brilliant, but they couldn't keep me hemmed in all the time. Growing up too fast, the downtown drugstore became my new play-pen. Traditionally, high school kids hung out at the drugstore. We had two—one on each corner—separated by railroad tracks. The juniors and seniors hung out at McGregor's and the freshmen and sophomores hung out across the tracks at Morel's.

My goal was to be the center of any social gathering. We girls who lived in town had more opportunities to get together. Yet I had friends who lived out in the country, too. We all socialized at school but those who lived on the farms didn't get to do as much as us "town folk." I loved visiting my girlfriends' farms. One of my favorite adventures was going to Emily's house to pick peanuts and watch television. My family didn't have a TV set yet. Emily had television; I had the drugstore hangout. I wondered if Emily and the other farm kids envied me as they passed the drugstore in the afternoons. Did they gaze out the bus window and long to be there, too?

Main Street Junior High was a sprawling old brick building, probably built before World War II. The high school was a two-story pre-World War I red brick building, which my mother attended in the early '20s. The two schools were a block away from each other. The main street of our little town was teeming with kids at three o'clock when the school bell rang for dismissal.

After school the eighth graders scurried like insects for the side-walks to town. Hordes of teenagers jammed the three-foot sidewalks with one thing in mind—ice cold coke. The bus kids hung out the windows, waving and hollering at their friends.

We loved to walk the three blocks to Morel's Drugstore. We must have looked like an army of ants as we piled into the store. The owner cowered in the recesses of the store—like he was afraid of us. We never noticed. We were only interested in getting there first to claim a seat on the chrome and Naugahyde barstools. Couples opted for the wire sweetheart-shaped chairs and round tables. Everybody's mouths were watering for an ice cold fountain drink or an ice cream sundae. Few of us had the money for anything more than a five cent coke and a pack of crackers.

The "railroad track gang" was not a gang in the sense of today's culture, but the clusters of kids who lived close to the tracks and walked to school together. Daddy drove a school bus. Sometimes on chilly mornings I got up early and rode the route with him. I flirted with the cute farm boys as they swaggered down the bus aisle. In warm weather I walked the mile and a half to school with the railroad track gang. I had my eye on high school aged twins, Ronald and Donald. They were almost sixteen. They "took me under their wings," saying they would look after me. We teased and joked. Some days Ronald worked after school bagging groceries, so I walked with Donald. I confided with him that I had a crush on his twin. Ronald was a "hunka hunka" varsity quarterback, short, but strong.

When fall came, I joined the eighth grade cheerleading squad. This gave me the privilege of riding on the athletic bus to the games—with Ronald. His thick blond hair fell over his ocean blue eyes. I swooned and fell head over heels for him.

Before long Ronald and I were going steady. High school got out ten minutes earlier so he would walk to the end of the junior high sidewalk and wait for me. Kids teased Ronald about liking an eighth grader, but he never let on that it bothered him.

We walked to Morel's together. Ronald found us a table and held out the chair for me—such a gentleman. Just like in the movies, I stole a glance at him. *Imagine me, with a high school boyfriend*, I thought. Grinning at me, I could see his pearly white, straight teeth. He looked sharp, dressed in a white button-down shirt, khakis, and dark brown leather lace-up shoes. He reminded me of the movie star, Alan Ladd in *Shane*.

We bent forward, heads touching, sipping soda—two straws in one Coca Cola glass—holding hands under the table. Someone always had a nickel or two to play the jukebox. Elvis Presley was the hottest sensation around. I had seen him once on the *Ed Sullivan Show*. With my eyes closed, I listened to Elvis croon, "Love Me Tender." Jerking me back to reality, Ronald asked, "How about a banana split?"

"Wow!" I exclaimed. *A banana split cost thirty-five cents—half of one hour of Ronald's wage!* He ordered the split. We hurried through it because my mother didn't like me dallying too long.

On our way home, we walked through the park to the railroad tracks. It was fun to try to balance on the rails, one foot in front of the other. As the track stretched towards Waycross, it cut deeper into the rise of the road. It was hard clay going straight up about ten feet as we neared his house. Climbing out of the embankment was not an easy feat for me in my calico full skirt and crinolines. I thought I looked like Marilyn Monroe in it. A woman never forgets her first high heels, tight skirt, or bra. It would be even tougher when it got cold enough for me to wear the one store-bought straight skirt I owned.

The Thomas's yard was like ours—no grass, just sandy soil. Ronald and I spent many hours standing in his yard until Mrs. Thomas called out that my mother was looking for me. Often I was barefoot, holding my ballerina slippers in my hand while twirling my toes in the sand. Ronald would then walk me the rest of the way home.

My parents enjoyed having Ronald around. They knew the Thomas's were good boys. I always thought Mama approved of Ronald because she graduated from high school with his daddy. Mr. Thomas was a rural mail carrier. The two of them joked around and had been good buddies all their lives. That made it okay for me to spend a lot of time at the Thomas's house.

Ronald and I met every Friday night at the skating rink a few miles down the road between Blackshear and Waycross. I loved the warm, balmy days at the rink. The crude hinged half walls folded back for the boys who came not for the skating, but for the girl watching. This was the only kind of air-conditioning available. The place wasn't much too look at—it hadn't been painted in years. But memories were made of this.

Some farm boys borrowed their dad's trucks and gathered around the ledge outside the rink to watch the girls skate. They would siphon off just enough gas from their daddy's farm tractor to get to the skating rink on Friday and Saturday nights. They leaned on the lower half walls and gawked at the cute girls as the song "I'm a Girl-Watcher" blared over the loudspeaker. Teenage boys showed up from the five surrounding counties just to do this. Those were the guys who couldn't skate or thought they were too macho to try. The lucky guys who were experienced skaters embraced their girls and circled the rink in time to the music. Some even showed off their dance tricks. But when they only had enough money for gas—at ten cents a gallon—there was always girl watching with the farm boys.

When it wasn't football season, I tried my best to never miss a Friday at the roller rink. If I could scrounge up enough money, I would go both Friday and Saturday night. I wasn't old enough to date yet, so we girls had to talk our fathers into dropping us off at the skating rink to flirt! That didn't mean just flirting with Ronald. It was open season. Any guy was fair game!

The best part of the evening was skating around the oval rink and smiling coyly at the cutest boys. Sometimes a breeze would rush through the rink, flipping up my short skate skirt. I imagined I was a skating star! I wasn't very good at backwards skating, but I tried anyway. Sometimes I lost my balance, tipping over a bit. This revealed the bloomers that just matched the color of the gold lining of my short skating skirt. All this was a tactic to get attention. I admit it—I was weaned on "chick flicks." Piper Laurie, Janet Leigh, and Doris Day were my heroes. I dreamed about being an actress all the time. I certainly didn't connect flirting with sex because we were clueless in those days. Nothing of a sexual nature was ever on television. It was a wholesome time when propriety and courtesy were important to a girl's reputation.

• • •

That summer in 1957 I was almost fourteen. It was easy to slip into car dating with Ronald because my family trusted him. I was one of the first girls in my class to actually do this. Probably because my parents knew Ronald so well.

My curfew was ten o'clock. Mama always joked, "If you are ever out after curfew, you'd better bring home the flat tire to prove it!" That meant I better have a good reason for being late.

A new dance place for teens had just opened up outside of town over the weekend. It was Sunday and I wanted to go, but we Methodists were not allowed to dance on Sunday. That made no sense to me. If we could dance any other day of the week, why not Sunday? Methodist Youth Fellowship (MYF) met at six o'clock followed by church. I usually met Ronald there and he took me home afterward. My parents never explained their feelings about this dancing taboo, but I knew the score. Don't ask!

So when Ronald said let's skip MYF and church and get a little dancing in at this new hot teen hangout, it sounded irresistible!

We sneaked off to Dowling's! The place was packed. Once we were inside the door we didn't give a second thought to where we were supposed to be . . . until the trip home.

We walked out to Ronald's old Ford. It was a warm summer night; the stars were popping on like Christmas lights. "The Twelfth of Never" was playing on the radio as we drove down the lonely two lane asphalt road from Dowling's back to town. Feeling dreamy, I leaned over and laid my head on his shoulder—just like the song says.

The night had been blissful—I didn't want it to end. But I had to be home by ten o'clock sharp!

BLAM! *Did someone fire a gun?* My heart was pounding under my white peasant blouse. "What's that?" Ronald didn't have time to answer.

Flap, flap.

"Dagnabbit, it's a blowout!" he said.

Uh oh, how are we going to make curfew now?

"Hurry, Ronald. I have got to get home by ten o'clock!"

"I'm trying," his voice was edgy. "Nuts! I don't have a jack!"

The darkness enveloped us as we contemplated our predicament. Was God laughing?

Finally, a buddy of Ronald's came by on his way home from Dowling's. He had a jack and the guys set to work. They struggled with the lug nuts on the 1949 Ford which were rusty and on too tight! Looked like fate had us in the lurch.

Guiltily, I thought about how I should have been in church.

When we finally got home it was almost eleven o'clock. Sitting in front of my house, sweating over what to tell my folks, Ronald looked out the window. "Fiona, your old man is standing at the door in his drawers! We better go in and face the music!"

The front porch light snapped on.

"Get in here and see your mother, young lady." He motioned me to their bedroom. Daddy could give you a look that would freeze a fire. I was too scared to be embarrassed by how silly Daddy looked with his knobby knees poking out beneath his boxer shorts. Ronald followed me into my parents' bedroom. We stood at attention at the foot of the bed. Stammering, I tried to explain about the flat tire. Ronald filled in where he could.

"Well, we got the flat tire outside, Mrs. Graham," Ronald began.

"Yes Mama, didn't you say that I should bring the flat tire home if I ever was late?" I asked, trying to muster a little humor. Silence. It didn't work.

We were cowering at the foot of their bed in the dark—waiting for the boom to drop!

Daddy announced, "No show and tell. Ronald, time for you to go home, son."

"Daddy," I began to stammer. "But, but, but—the flat tire."

They didn't believe us! Could they tell that we had been dancing? Would I be grounded forever?

I was often surprised at how savvy my parents were when it came to teenagers. That explains why they opened their own teenage hangout the next spring. Eventually I told them the truth about that night. That old guilt gets me every time. Fiona's first flat tire is now a family joke.

4

Order Out of Chaos

All of my life I have liked things to be orderly. Perhaps it's because I was the only one in my family who liked to maintain order. My parents and sister were famous for their clutter. For as long ago as I can remember I have tried to clean up after them. Even after marrying and moving to Atlanta, I still found myself straightening their things. In fact, whenever something was missing my mother would ask me to find it—even if that meant calling me in Atlanta after I had returned from visiting her. She just came to expect that I had picked up the item she was looking for and put it away somewhere.

It wasn't always just Mama's things. My sister was as untidy as I was tidy. Can you imagine the bedroom we shared together growing up? We had matching dressers that sat side by side in our room. Everything was organized in my two drawers. The top drawer was for treasures and keepsakes. I kept my panties, undershirts, and slips inside my bottom drawer—all lined up and divided into sections. My sister's dresser, on the other hand, was a complete disaster. Closing her dresser drawers was like trying to push a trick snake back into its can. Was this the sign of two very different personalities? I have to cut my sister some slack—she was four years younger than me.

Between the ages of eight and thirteen, I spent a lot of time after school with Mama in the family store. To take advantage of the time when business was slow, my mother hemmed a dress or solved crossword puzzles. Daddy moved her Singer sewing machine to the store so she could sew school clothes for my sister and me. The corner of the storefront became cluttered with stacks of patterns and scraps of fabric. It looked so messy, it drove me nuts. Straightening those patterns became my entertainment.

Sometimes when I would get frustrated with the sewing corner I reverted to stocking the shelves. That posed an opportunity for success. The plugs of tobacco, cans of snuff, and canned goods were easier to keep in order than the crumpled patterns. Standing back, I puffed up with pride hoping folks would notice the neat rows of products. No one ever asked who had stacked the goods, but I imagined that they liked my work.

When old magazines and newspapers would get shoved under the glass candy display shelf, I fixed them. I stacked those over and over each day while drooling over the unwrapped jawbreakers, malted milk balls, and jellied orange slices. After fifteen minutes or so, I would ask Mama if I could have a Tootsie Roll, being careful to say "may I" instead of "can I."

"Are you going to eat all of your supper tonight?"

"Yes, ma'am!" I knew the right answers.

Five minutes later I asked for a jawbreaker. This went on for many an afternoon. Sometimes I got a lot of candy. It depended on how distracted Mama was when I asked. These little rewards undoubtedly reinforced my desire to straighten things.

Cutting and measuring fabric to make clothes also seemed to satisfy my need for orderliness. One day Mama allowed me to cut out a circular skirt for myself. Sewing lessons with Mama always started with spreading the cloth over the store counter, a perfect place to cut out the fabric. Together she and I arranged the tissue paper pattern over the fabric, smoothing it out so the corners matched just so. I placed the pins neatly, exactly twelve inches apart. I could daydream about being a movie star like Esther Williams, while doing these mundane tasks. I wasn't a brunette, but I wanted to be.

At times I stood looking at Mama's desk in the back of the store. It looked like a cyclone had been through. The tiny slips of paper Mama left lying around bugged me. I loved to hide them in a special cubby. Wanting to be helpful, I arranged the paper clips, put away the clutter, and stacked the countless papers.

Whenever it was too cold or dreary to play outside, I kept myself busy inside the store, straightening shelves. First, I would line up the different sized grocery bags under the front counter and tighten the strings around them. Next, I would wipe out the roach eggs and throw away the old newspapers. I was worried people might know about the roaches and decide not to buy our groceries.

When I was twelve Mama and Daddy paid me fifty cents an hour to bag groceries, serve the customers, and sweep up at closing time. I added up each item on the adding machine, accepted payments, and made change. No computer told me how much money to give back. Most of our customers only bought a few groceries at a time and charged them until payday. It was my job to write down the details of what they bought. Once I completed their order form, I would give them the pink copy and put the white one in the cash drawer. An air of self-importance blossomed in my mind. Getting paid made it even better. Fifty cents an hour was a lot of money. I used it to buy my shoes, coat, and any special things I wanted for the school year.

When I was fourteen, our family store was converted into Graham's Dari Kream. We served soft ice cream as well as short order hot dogs,

French fries, and hamburgers. I still made it my job to straighten under the counters.

As an adult, I continue to like order but I am not as consistent in maintaining it. I spend half my time creating disorder and the other half trying to fix it. Sometimes I wonder if the fact that I'm a June baby has anything to do with my dual personality traits. Some people call it Gemini. Maybe my Gemini personality has always been there and I'm just becoming more aware of it. Certainly the contradiction and fickleness of my lifestyle supports this claim. Nowadays, one boot gets thrown into the corner and the other slides under the bed. Half of me wants to throw caution to the wind, relax and be "laid back" while the other half wants everything put neatly in its place—order out of chaos. Since I became blind, though, I've realized how much I need order. Disorder can be my own worst enemy. Creating systems for being organized is a necessity, a necessary evil for me.

To this day, whenever I am worried, analyzing a situation, or feeling sad, I go to my closet or my chest of drawers and rearrange everything. I enjoy solving problems in my head while putting things in order. As I fold, straighten, and set things back in their proper place, I know that when the next week comes, my Gemini self will resurface and I'll go back to throwing things on the floor or tossing them in the closet. The room will be a cluttered mess again in a month. By then, I will have a new problem to solve so the process will start all over again.

You can see my transformation from messy to neat comes with my mood. When Jerry and I fight and I don't talk to him for days, he breaks the ice by calling me and asking, "What drawer are you straightening tonight?"

If it were not for my life challenges, my room would be an utter disaster.

5

Dose of Reality

When I was nineteen years old Pierce County opened a hospital in Blackshear. It was a clay-colored brick building with two wings—one for White people and the smaller wing for Colored. (*Colored* was the generally accepted word for Negroes in the South.) Although no one ever pointed this out, we knew this was segregation. The first wing had a nurses' station and twenty rooms. The other wing had two or three rooms plus the emergency room, X-ray lab, and kitchen.

In 1962 central air conditioning was only available in such new buildings—most people had window units. Summers were long and hot in South Georgia. The prospect of working in a cool environment appealed to me in more ways than one. I needed to work and I was tired of working for my parents in the Dari Kream slinging hamburgers. I wanted something different, more sophisticated.

After one year at a small two year college, I was no closer to knowing what I wanted to be when I grew up than when I started. My friends were moving away, taking jobs at the beach. Some even went as far as South Carolina to a resort hotel. That sounded very glamorous. Being a movie buff, I was "into glamorous." Mama said, "Since you are trying to decide between nursing and teaching, why don't you apply for a job as a nurse's aide at the new hospital."

A nurse's aide takes temperatures and blood pressures, as well as feeds and bathes the patients. She makes beds, cleans rooms, and empties bedpans. Not as exciting or glamorous as working at a resort, but I wanted to see if I had the temperament to work with sick people.

I knew my parents would discourage me from going away to some exotic place like Myrtle Beach, the home of shag dancing. Not their little girl! My obedient nature just wouldn't let me be adventurous.

The hospital was only five minutes from my house. After filling out the application, they hired me on the spot! I didn't know how badly they needed bedpan engineers. Taking the hospital job meant getting up at six o'clock in the morning five days a week. My pay was $1.05 per hour. At the end of the day, I rushed home and made a beeline for my bed. My poor feet hurt so badly!

Back in the '60s, nurse's aides were considered to be the general flunkies—doing what the nurse didn't want to do such as cleaning bedpans and urinals. It was grueling work, but I didn't care. I loved the order of it all. It was the first step to a medical career. In my nineteen-year-old perspective I was paying my dues.

Making my daily rounds, I walked alone down the hall with my clipboard and blood pressure cuff in hand. My crepe sole shoes squeaked as I moved with purpose in my crisp blue and white uniform. Putting on a broad smile, I greeted each patient with a cheery, "How are you today?" I felt important. My patients needed me.

During my first week at the hospital, I was called to the emergency room for a difficult childbirth. "They might need your help," said the nurse at the station.

Me, help? I thought to myself. I didn't know a thing about birthing.

When I arrived I saw a very young, tiny black woman squatting over an army green metal trash can. The nurses were fussing at her. "You should have made arrangements to see a doctor. If you had done so, you wouldn't be in this predicament."

The nursing staff whispered to each other, shaking their heads and clucking about how the woman had nine months to prepare for this baby. Amid the chaos, I heard the nurses say it wasn't going well. The baby was breech—complications I didn't understand. Since she had no money and no doctor, they did not want to admit her. Was there a policy not to take indigent people? How could they turn her away? I stared, shocked. This was my first personal experience with prejudice and I didn't like it.

"How cruel!" I whispered to myself, afraid to be heard.

Biting my lower lip, I stared as the woman writhed in pain and squatted over the trash can, trying to grunt that baby out. After what seemed like an hour, someone with authority arrived and whisked her away. I didn't know where she was taken. I didn't ask . . . I just kept my mouth shut. I often wondered how that baby came into this world—in a sterile delivery room or in a dirty trash can.

Times were certainly different back in the early '60s. Midwives had no training, just experience. Black people rarely saw doctors. As I learned much later from my veterinarian father-in-law, doctors in his profession mainly treated black folks. I found that appalling, but that's the way it was.

One day the nurses told me we had a new cancer patient—the "big C." Cancer was rare in those days and people said the word in a hushed manner. I could tell which room he was in by the stench that permeated the hallway outside his door. This man was dying and it was our job to make him comfortable in the process. No one could do anything more. We didn't have the Angels of Mercy (hospice) in those days. I dreaded the day when it was my turn to care for him.

One evening I arrived and found my turn had come to take care of this old, old man in Room 113. He looked ancient. Entering his room, I held my breath. The stench was overwhelming. The shock of seeing this rotting bag of shriveled flesh and bones stopped me dead in my tracks. I didn't think he saw me standing at the foot of his bed. The room was as still as a cemetery except for the whir of his oxygen tank. A tent covered the top half of his body. Looking around, my eyes widened and I sucked in air. I prayed that he didn't hear me. His labored breathing indicated he was in great distress and I wondered about his pain level.

A couple weeks later I went in to check on him and noticed the oxygen tank was gone. This man looked so drawn and yellow against the white sheets. I imagined he was a huge vile puss pocket oozing over the sheets. His yellowish gray skin stretched taut over his bald head and bony face. Every time I came in to check his vitals, he had his mouth open. He looked so dead like that! I feared being the one to discover he had passed away. I had never seen someone die. *Please, God, don't let him die while I am in the room.* Trembling, I shook him slightly to take his temperature. Relief swept over me when his dead eyes opened and stared. He had lived one more day. But why?

Every night when I got off work, that man was on my mind. Who was his family? Where were they? Did anyone care? I couldn't really tell how old he was. Does cancer make you look older than you really are? Did the horrible smell mean he was rotting away inside?

The last night I saw the old man alive, it was business as usual. I sighed and forced myself to do what I could for him. I brought him a pitcher of fresh water. This ritual seemed silly—he never drank the water. I didn't realize that he couldn't reach it. I should have pressed it to his open lips. I didn't know. I just stared at him. When I touched him, he didn't move. *How dead he looks, but he can't be! I can hear his shallow breath.* I wanted to run out of the room and scream, "Somebody do something!" My heart squeezed tight like it was folding up on itself. I shrank from the cloud of death in that room. The image has haunted me for years.

Cancer meant you would die a miserable, ugly death and no one could save you. It reminded me of the plague which I read about in world history. A dreaded disease everyone was afraid of and no one could cure. I developed a secret fear of getting cancer that took years to get over.

One night I was given the task of going to the segregated wing of the hospital to bathe a severely crushed young black man—a timber accident victim. A huge pine tree had fallen on him, leaving his right side crushed. Delirious much of the time, the nurses said he had brain damage.

They didn't want to bother with this young colored man who spent most of his time screaming or talking out of his head. Prejudice was alive in South Georgia. I didn't know why I was sent to care for this young pulpwood worker (the term was "pulpwood nigger" in that day), but now I believe it was because no one else wanted to do that kind of work.

I had grown up around black people all my life. We lived on the main street of town, which backed up to their community. My mother prepared their income taxes and read the government letters to those who could not read. She was well respected and known all her life by many of these folks. I had no reason to fear or feel prejudice as many others did. I had always been taught to treat everyone with respect and dignity.

Standing in the doorway, I took one look at my new charge on the segregated wing and my eyes filled with tears. He writhed in pain and mumbled something I couldn't understand. His skin was dark brown and crusty with dried blood. His head, still matted with blood, had a white bandage around it. *How much care had gone into cleaning this patient?* I wondered. Walking to his sink, I filled a pan with warm sudsy water and sat on the edge of his bed. Dipping the thin white washcloth in the water, I gently rubbed away the dried blood from his arm. After a long time and multiple water changes, I felt satisfied that his body was clean and called for the orderly to take care of his private parts. I had been nervous, but it went well. He didn't even stir. I think the gentle washing calmed him as he drifted in and out of consciousness. I guess because I did such a good job they sent me in there every day to take care of his needs.

Driving home that night, I couldn't stop thinking about why I had such trouble getting this man clean. At first I thought it was because he must have gotten awfully dirty during his accident. But, what was so perplexing to me was that each time I rubbed his arm small brown flecks clung to the washcloth. I went home that night and told my mother.

"Mama, I can't get this boy clean."

"What do you mean?"

"Every time I scrub him, there are more brown flecks."

Mama smiled. "Honey, that is the dead skin flaking off."

I didn't know our skin did that. We were so creamy white that it didn't show up on our washcloths. No wonder I couldn't tell if I was getting him clean.

"Poor man! I bet I have rubbed him raw!"

On the third day the pulpwood worker started mumbling again. Although I couldn't understand him, I knew he spoke Geechee because our maid from South Carolina spoke the same language. Indeed, this young man was from the Lowcountry region of South Carolina near the coast.

The next day I was going about my business, cleaning his room and making up the bed, when he suddenly sat up in his bed. Alert for the first time, he grabbed my wrist with his good hand and mumbled a girl's name. I was startled. He must have thought I was his girlfriend. I managed to wriggle loose and ring for help. When the orderly arrived, I simply told him to take over. I was too scared to go back inside. Intellectually I knew that he didn't know what he was doing, but I had never had a man grab me like that. His eyes were wild and desperate.

I was disgusted with myself for not going back into his room and disappointed with the rest of the staff for shunning him. After a few days, I mustered enough courage to check on him. He was much more lucid so we spent some time together talking about his girlfriend. Three days after that I walked into his room and he was gone. I rushed to the nurse's station to determine his whereabouts, but they just shrugged their shoulders.

My last experience at the hospital was administering Trilene to a patient in labor. Trilene was the anesthesia of the era. Actually it was obsolete according to my friend, Linda, who was studying to become a nurse. She was shocked when I told her I was asked to administer anesthesia to a patient.

"Well, I declare, an aide giving ether!" stammered my nurse friend.

"It's a small hospital, so there was no one else to do it," I replied.

Everybody was waiting around when I entered the delivery room. I immediately recognized the patient as someone I knew from high school.

"Where is the doctor?"

"Oh, he is at home watching the ball game. We will call him when she gets close," said someone from the delivery team.

What if something goes wrong? Will he be able to get here in time? Answering my own questions, I reminded myself that nothing is far away in Blackshear and there is never any traffic.

I set about doing the prep work as instructed. It was my first time shaving anything other than my own legs. Here I was rubbing down and shaving the huge belly of a high school friend. We weren't even close friends. I felt bad that this was my job and I knew she must have been embarrassed. Trying to keep up a light, cheery conversation to set her at ease, I shaved her belly smooth—all the while praying that I wouldn't nick her.

Finally the doctor arrived. I sighed with relief, figuring the game was over. Without much instruction, he told me to give her ether as needed. Every time I saw pain on her face I clasped the cup over her nose and mouth. This was serious business.

I marveled at the playfulness of the delivery team while they stood over the patient. The doctor told a joke and everyone laughed. It was just as though the patient wasn't there. Suddenly the doctor's voice broke through the laughter. "You have given her too much ether! She is knocked out. She can't help push," he said looking directly at me.

"I didn't know!" I stammered. "Sorry."

Despite the fact that I gave the mother too much ether and made her sick, the baby finally decided to come on its own. I don't even remember if it was a boy or a girl. I was just relieved that the baby was healthy and my job was complete.

Now, to my amazement, while the doctor was stitching up her vagina (a procedure called a perineotomy) he started to sing. "Tie me perinea down, sport . . ."—a parody of a popular Australian song. If the patient had been awake, I'm certain she would not have found it funny.

Although each day at the hospital was a new adventure, I decided that I truly did not have the stamina for the medical field. Today the medical profession has clinical nurse assistants (CAN) and techs as the orderlies. When I was working as a nurse's aide in the '60s, I took temperatures, administered medicines, and did many of the things skilled medical personnel do today. Back then, there were no LPNs and not enough registered nurses to do the work. I hardly lasted five weeks working at my hometown's hospital, but it left me with strong impressions of birth, prejudice, and death at the tender age of nineteen. These visions will remain like cobwebs in my brain for the rest of my life.

6

Mama Got Liberated at the P.W.

A successful tax preparation business had grown out of the bookkeeping business Mama had run for as long as I can remember. At seventy, she was making money hand over fist. Mama and Daddy never had the money to adapt a car for her. I doubt she ever expressed interest in getting something like that. Hand gears on a car were a recent development in the '70s. Besides, Daddy took her everywhere she wanted to go.

Mama had a secret desire to drive all of her life. One day, Mama got a wild hair and ordered her life's dream—a car of her own. She told no one of her plan, not even Daddy. She ordered it on the phone. When a white Toyota station wagon pulled up into the carport, Daddy came out of the Dari Kream to see what was happening. Mama proudly announced that the car would be adapted and she would be taking driving lessons soon.

"Sweetheart, you have always had me to drive and you always will!"

Now she made this decision without consulting Daddy. She had never done anything without his knowledge. They discussed everything. I don't know what got into my mother. A late midlife crisis? I wasn't there, but they must have talked at length. The next I heard was that she had canceled the hand gears and lessons. Daddy loved cars, so the car stayed. Since Paige, my niece, was old enough to drive, she began driving Miss Nana around town. Mama would have a little independence after all. Still, I know she was disappointed. My mother never expressed how she felt. As a marriage partner, she knew the right thing to do. Respecting her husband's wishes, she did not fight Daddy about this. I didn't agree with this but it was her decision.

Just nine years later, Daddy was getting in the car to take his "bride" for a ride—something he did on a daily basis. Putting his hand on the door handle, he looked over at Nana and said, "Do you mind if we don't go today?"

"No, of course not."

"I think I just need to sit down." Daddy walked back into the house and sat down on the sofa.

Mama rolled in behind him. "Kenny, are you all right?"

Daddy didn't answer—he just fell forward onto the floor.

Mama jumped out of her wheelchair and crawled over to Daddy. She tried to lift him back onto the sofa but couldn't. Reaching for the telephone, she pulled it off the counter and called 9-1-1. Daddy died five days later.

Before Daddy died, he was making arrangements to get Mama an electric wheelchair. She had used a push wheelchair ever since she had a stroke in 1988. I often wondered if she regretted not learning to drive.

My sister lived near Mama and checked on her daily. Sandra sold advertising for the radio station. One day she needed to pick up the supermarket ad for the week. She knew Mama and Daddy had a daily routine of going to the Piggly Wiggly supermarket in Waycross to meet and greet their friends. "Mama, I have to call on the manager at the Piggly Wiggly. Why don't you ride over with me?"

Mama never missed a chance to get out. She rolled out to the car and hopped in because she couldn't get the wheelchair close enough.

When Sandra and she entered the store, they noticed a new amenity for customers. A motorized shopping cart—a comfortable chair with a basket and joystick. It looked inviting. With a twinkle in her eye, she told my sister, "Hold that chair still while I get on. I am going for a test drive!"

Sandra wasn't given any time to protest. She knew Mama didn't have the legs for balance and it was quite a stretch from the seat to the joystick.

Mama only saw *freedom*! She transferred herself over, palmed the joystick, and felt the power! My mother had never used a joystick before and didn't realize how sensitive it was until it was too late. She gave it a little push.

"Ooooweee! Bye Sandra." She had that Richard Petty look in her eye! All Mama needed was a helmet and driving gloves.

Not waiting for my sister's response, Mama raced up the first aisle, narrowly missing a customer. Her start was a little jerky, but she never looked back. Racing down the next aisle, she waved to Sandra. My sister stood there, openmouthed. Wearing high heels, she was not going to chase her mother down. Trying to act like this was normal, she strode over to speak to the manager who was stocking an endcap display.

The two stood in front of a huge pyramid of L'eggs panty hose. They chatted as Sandra watched out of the corner of her eye for her wayward mother.

Rounding the bend with intent, Mama picked up a passenger in the back of the store next to the bacon. The six foot tall pink pig dressed in a ruffled apron had a smile on her face, a yellow curly wig, and a black frying pan in her hand. The sign read: "Bring home the bacon tonight!" Mama clipped the edge of the cardboard statue as she made her turn. Mrs. Pig bounced along behind Mama, attached to the wild woman's electric cart.

Chatting with Bob, the manager, Sandra looked up to see Mama making her way towards them. Sandra gasped, causing Bob to look behind him. The two froze in disbelief. Mama had a look of pure excitement. She was coming right for them. The joystick wobbled and Mama had no idea of how to control it. Bob laughed and Sandra giggled nervously. Their expression changed when she cut the pair off. Sandra lost her balance and fell towards the pyramid of L'eggs. The manager tried to break her fall by reaching out to help. Both of them stumbled into the display. L'eggs panty hose eggs started their avalanche. They tumbled and rolled.

Sandra and Bob recovered as Sandra stammered, "Mama, come back. Stop!" Sandra and the store manager were picking up the fallen L'eggs as Mama waved confidently, on the next turn.

Mama had ignored Sandra's cries of panic. On her final lap, she slowed to a stop. Grinning broadly, "Sandra, I'm ready for my own wheels! Order that new electric Hoveround which Daddy wanted me to have."

That's how Mama got liberated at the P.W.

Acknowledgments

My grateful thanks goes out to the many people who encouraged me and cared for me through the past twenty-four years. So many appeared, some for brief moments, and nudged me along my journey from a shattered life to one with true vision.

A special thanks to Judy Dodge who assisted me, traveled with me, listened to me, and helped me develop my speaking career. Thanks, Judy, for the weary tour nights when you closed the day with, "Fiona, do you want me to read to you?"

Marcia West, I could not have taken this writing journey without you. Listening to me rant and rave, you teased me, encouraged me, and kept me going with your friendship and your work as my special editor.

Thanks to Carolyn Curtis and Lindsay Bridges who came along to add the finishing touches like icing on a cake.

I am grateful to all three of you for your fine editing.

My appreciation goes out to Doug Shiver for his artistic talent with the book cover, his wise choice of the subtitle, and his friendship.

Charles Cochran deserves credit for the intriguing title. It was a brilliant moment when he turned to me and said, "Your nightlife is all day, every day."

I do live in total darkness. Thank you, Charles, for your ideas and encouragement.

The Light That Is Fiona

John Rice is a published author and wise friend. He and his wife have been my friends for over twenty-eight years. John wrote this poem about me the day I lost my sight. He is ninety-three years old and resides in an assisted living home where he enjoys telling stories to the other residents. John composed and recorded this as a song too.

A rose does not see, yet its beauty we see
    Receiving of nothing, its beauty is free,
Giving of self in sightless wonder,
    Giving us praise, 'tis a shrine we would ponder,
A gift from life's garden for us who can see.

A jewel sees not, yet its luster we see,
    Shining with splendor that it does not see,
Giving of sparkling reflections bright,
    Creation's gift of value and light,
A gift from the earth for us who can see.

A rainbow sees not while its colors we see,
    'Tis lavish in colors for all who can see –
Sky-mounted in glory, the thunder cloud's fleece
    A gift from on high, the promise of peace
That follows the darkest of storms that we see.

A candle sees not while its light we do see,
    Receiving of naught as it lights what we see,
Giving itself in sacrifice burning –
    Like unto valor, that sacrifice burning
Giving of self to light what we see.

Bright candle of valor, bright rainbow at sea,
  Dear jewel and sweet rose in Fiona we see.
In courage unmeasured, defying the dark,
  On a sea of concern bravely sailing her barque,
She smiles for the world and for us who can see.

'Tis she whose patience makes misery flee,
  Forbidding its presence with us who can see –
No light of more valor, no color more fair,
  No luster more prized, no beauty more rare,
Than that which in lovely Fiona we see.

Shine on, dear Fiona, for you are the key
  That can open the windows that help us to see
What power there is in a heart of love
  That is lifting bruised eyes to angels above.
In time, dear Fiona, in time you will see.

These wonders unseeing are gifts that are free.
  From us they ask nothing, to us they are free;
And we who ask much, seeing light everyday,
  Give never as well or as freely as they,
And they go on giving to us who can see.

Shine on, dear Fiona, like a sun-spangled sea
  Though darkness abysmal forbids you to see
Though bruising of fell circumstance you inherit,
  Misfortune's foul beating is not your true merit.
Your face is a radiance to us who can see.

Shine on, dear Fiona, there's a mantle for thee;
  Rose, Jewel, Bright Rainbow, and Brave Candle to be.
Your darkness will never bedim your sweet light.
  You always will brighten your world and your night.
In time, dear Fiona, in time you will see.

Shine on, dear Fiona, there's a mantle for thee;
   Rose, Jewel, Bright Rainbow, and Brave Candle to be.
Your darkness will never bedim your sweet light.
   You always will brighten your world and your night.
In time, dear Fiona, in time you will see.